Editors
Travis Denton & Katie Chaple

International Editor
Thomas Lux

Layout & Design
Travis Denton

Special Thanks to
Poetry@TECH,
the School of Literature, Media and Communication
and Georgia Tech's Ivan Allen College

terminus is published with generous support from

Poetry@TECH
www.poetry.gatech.edu

terminus seeks to publish the most thought-provoking, socially and culturally aware writing available. While we want to push the boundaries of general aesthetics and standards, we also want to publish writing that is accessible to a wide audience. We seek to live up to the highest standards in publishing, always growing and reaching new levels of understanding and awareness both within our immediate community and within the greater communities of our country and world. *terminus* accepts unsolicited submissions year-round, but keep in mind that most of our content is solicited. We encourage simultaneous submissions, so long as we are notified. Address all correspondence to: *terminusmagazine@gmail.com*.

a Poetry@TECH
sponsored publication

terminus is printed by Lightning Source and distributed by Ingram.

ISBN: 978-0-9909961-1-8

The *terminus* logo was designed by Natalie Farr

Front & Back Covers, inside covers, insert and all things artsy
by Lawrence Yang

Front Cover: *Curious Giraffe*. Ink, watercolor, & gouache on paper, 5"x 5"
Inside Cover: *Sleep with the Fishes*. Ink, watercolor, & gouache on paper, 10"x 18"
Back Cover: *Rooster Tree*. Ink, watercolor, & gouache on paper, 9"x 12"

We recommend you check out more
of Lawrence Yang's work online at
www.suckatlife.com

Contents

Featuring
Poetry@TECH's 2014-15 Visiting Poets

Art

Poetry

Campbell McGrath

Guadalcanal (1942)

In his diary, Second Lieutenant Yasuo Ko'o, color bearer of the 124th Infantry, Japanese Imperial Army, recorded an unfailing formula with which he calibrated the life expectancy of his fellows in the last days of 1942:

> *Those who can stand—30 days*
> *Those who can sit up—3 weeks*
> *Those who cannot sit up—1 week*
> *Those who urinate lying down—3 days*
> *Those who have stopped speaking—2 days*
> *Those who have stopped blinking—tomorrow*

> *—Richard B. Frank, Guadalcanal*

Awakened from dreams of rice cakes and candy
by a small frog jumping onto my face.
These creatures are known to be poisonous,
else we would certainly eat them,
if any of us remain strong enough to catch one.

Not Basho's frog, this strange citizen of the jungle—
watching his slim body swell with each breath
what I feel is not curiosity but envy.

When I climb to my feet my head swims
as if drunk on new year's whiskey,
I hold to a tree hoping these currents will subside
but there is no respite from this symptom,
hardly the worst of our afflictions.

These rugged cliffs resemble ink drawings
by some ancient Chinese master.
Was it another lifetime in which I sat sketching
mountains along the Kikuchi River?
Yet the discipline of *tanka*, I discover, perseveres
even in the face of starvation and disease.

    Gentle brother frog,
        your jungle shows no mercy
  to weary soldiers
        fighting for the Emperor
        here—so far from Mount Kuju!

Images sustain me as I walk, passing before my eyes
and flowing in memory as in a dream—
clam-diggers in the shallows of the Inland Sea,
kites shaped like bees and carp above my native village,
the ocean a swath of blue silk printed with golden flowers—
until I am summoned back by hunger pangs,
by the fetor of death here on Starvation Island.

Yesterday we dug up buds of areca palms
but there is no nourishment in their fiber
and it is weeks since we have seen a grain of rice.
Salt—my body cries out for it and I vow
to drink a mouthful of seawater
should I survive to see the ocean once again.

Furukama, Nonoyama, Kawai, Takagi—
these men we left behind yesterday, too weak to walk.
Goro attempted suicide; his wound festers,
soon he will embrace the peace he sought.

Long ago we abandoned our steel helmets,
rifles, gas masks, binoculars—skin and bones,
even the strap of an empty canteen causes agony.

Our last grenade we threw into the river,
greedily devouring the small silver fish
killed in the blast, bones boiled with wild potato vines
as soup the next morning, our final meal,
how many days past, how many?

Today I bury my pistol in a sandy bank,
keeping only my katana as final recourse.

When we come to a bridge strongly-built
of hewn logs by our naval engineers
we are so weak that many men fall off.
I tumble into chest-deep water,
struggle through the current, holding fast.

Beneath a large tree on the far shore
we discover the engineers—
dead of starvation, decomposing,
consumed by the pervasive and intolerable rot.

Uemara can walk no further. I assure him
the relief party is on its way to this very bridge.
Do not leave this spot, Uemara—
you will be first to receive the rice
and canned beef as they come up the trail!

Some of the men grumble at his good fortune,
calling back as they resume the march.
Tell them which way we went, Uemara!
Don't let them forget about us, Uemara!

Of course there is no relief party—
the transports have been intercepted
and sunk by American warplanes.
All that can sustain us now is duty,
divine fortune, and the will to survive.

Starvation Island—
    as our ships drew near we cheered
the sight of your shores!
        How few will watch them vanish,
        bright with moonlight, sailing home.

The Coltrane Changes (1964)

John Coltrane is flying
further into the darkness
trying to learn why it sings,
why it sparkles and hearkens

at the plunge of a valve,
at the throb of a string,
Coltrane is trying
to learn everything, to solve

for the enharmonic unknown
within his own heart,
hurtling toward sainthood
scarred and enlightened and bent

at every joint, every staff or bar
he's ever been wounded by,
called by the dark star
of art to witness, and testify.

Apollo (1969)

This would be the vessel of our dismantling,
whose flames propose to outshine the divine
as science declares itself nemesis to myth.

What is science but a wondrous supposition
to shield yourselves from chaos, to explain,
as we once did, the order of the universe?

No, Helios' chariot does not transport the sun—
is that why you came, to steal his horses?
Is that why you voyaged to this negligible rock?

Earth, too, is a stone in a sea of darkness,
and now you are orphaned there, marooned
within your poisoned atmosphere of reason.

Destroying us will not reduce your insignificance.
Selene, that beautiful dreamer, will not vanish
because you plant a banner on her orb.

Did you think the moon her residence?
Fools. She lives where all gods do, as everything
you exalt and rage against does: in you.

Campbell McGrath's most recent collection of poems is his 2012 book *In the Kingom of the Sea Monkeys*, which was preceded by *Shannon, Seven Notebooks, Capitalism, American Noise, Spring Comes to Chicago, Road Atlas, Florida Poems,* and *Pax Atomica*. His awards include the Kingsley Tufts Poetry Award and fellowships from the Guggenheim and MacArthur Foundations. He teaches in the creative writing program at Florida International University in Miami.

James May

Gratis

Poets are not often rich, but this one was
since he embraced the state, wrote
doctrinal hymns, odes to celebrate
the dictator's birthday, even the dictator's dog.

So when another poet's daughter
went to see this poet—her father, a member
of the resistance movement, had been captured
in the woods and sentenced to death—

she did not expect sympathy. But still,
she told him, you're both poets,
and maybe this is worth something
(I don't know if she used a question mark).

I heard this story in the country where it happened.
I was drinking strong coffee. My friend
sipped white wine. Of course the one poet
used his political pull to save the other;

otherwise his reply to the daughter,
Well, what is poetry for but to save lives
(I don't know if he used a question mark either)
wouldn't have been remembered.

Nor would it have survived for decades
in the conversations of so many others
to reach me, who offered to pick up the check
only when he saw it securely in his friend's hand.

Penis

The word always looks absurd,
but especially when holding my own
as I piss and read the blue ink aching
over the flakes of chafed whitewash.

Such settings make all handwriting
seem juvenile, while my mind
goes back to the day Mrs. Bowling,
our sub, heard the first of us start our game.

You had to wait until her back was turned,
then yell "penis" as loud as you could
without getting caught. Then the kid next to you
had to do the same, only louder.

Some would smuggle it in their coughs;
the brave would belt it from the conch shell
of their folded hands. And when there was no doubt
of what we were doing, she turned,

not red-faced like we'd wanted,
nor was she holding back tears
like that twenty-something blonde before her
who was replaced by the headmaster

telling us all to feel bad, though most of us never did.
O wise and venerable Mrs. Bowling,
thank you for your calm indifference,
the look that taught at least some of us

that simply having a prick is no excuse
for being one. But years later,
I see there was more to our game
than just meanness. Here it is again, alone,

without an adjective to describe it, nor a verb
to put it in motion, erased a million times
from a million walls, authored by so many
who wanted to write this and only this,

as if writing the word would satisfy
whatever made us shout out so loudly,
hoping to be heard, but never caught
or held accountable, or worse: ignored.

James Davis May's poems have appeared or are forthcoming in Five Points, The Missouri Review, New England Review, New Ohio Review, The New Republic, Pleiades, Rattle, The Southern Review *and elsewhere. He has received scholarships from The Sewanee Writers' Conference, Inprint, and the Krakow Poetry Seminar. In 2013, he won the Collins Award from* Birmingham Poetry Review. *The former editor of* New South, *he is an assistant professor of English and Creative Writing at Young Harris College in Georgia.*

Joseph Millar

Roses

for Sierra

If you don't show up today
you will miss the fountain
shedding its torn shroud
over and over,
the baby asleep
in her yellow dress
and the flame-shaped conifers
near the entrance
smelling of last night's rain.

It's early Easter and no one
has seen him
since they rolled back the stone,
not even the Magdalene.
Is he in heaven, is he in hell
hiding among the roses?
The red ones that cover the arbor
or the ones dyed blue
that arrived in the night
sent by some secret admirer
no one will tell you the name of?

Maybe he's watched you leave home
each day, carrying your shoes in a bag:
the red ones for running,
the brown ones for work.
Maybe he follows you to the bus stop,

then walks through the Natural History Museum
gazing up at the skeleton of the whale,
its jaws and its flukes, its ribcage,
trying to imagine the size of its heart,
then sits in the Dollar movies alone
like a lover who can't forget you.

Memphis

Cleaning charred grease
from the barbecue

two days till the Fourth of July,
with Otis singing

"These Arms of Mine," scratchy
voice breaking the notes in half.

No one else home in the afternoon,
tool shed, shovel, iron rake.

Something only the dog can hear
faint like the wind

blowing over the fields,
the distant fireworks like gunfire:

planet of okra and green tomatoes,
planet of prisons and meth.

In Memphis the sun sets
over the pavements, over

the horn-lines of trumpet and sax:
falsetto, backbeat, wah-wah pedal,

lavender eggshell Coupe de Ville.
Black mystery train

pulling out of the station
sixteen coaches long.

Joseph Millar's first collection, Overtime *was a finalist for the 2001 Oregon Book Award. His second collection,* Fortune, *appeared in 2007, followed by a third,* Blue Rust, *in 2012.*

Millar grew up in Pennsylvania and attended Johns Hopkins University before spending 25 years in the San Francisco Bay area working at a variety of jobs, from telephone repairman to commercial fisherman. It would be two decades before he returned to poetry.

He has won fellowships from the John Simon Guggenheim Foundation and the National Endowment for the Arts, as well as a 2008 Pushcart Prize and has appeared in such magazines as DoubleTake, TriQuarterly, The Southern Review, APR, *and* Ploughshares. *Millar teaches in Pacific University's low-residency MFA.*

Adrienne Su

The Frost Place

Franconia, New Hampshire

The poets drank and declaimed outside
while I stayed in, tied to my body,

recalling, with minimal bitterness,
high school, its odd kisses, missing the party.

At least I had Frost, or the idea of Frost,
to talk to in the dark. And I'd bought

good maternity clothes, culled from racks
so flower-drenched, so vague, I thought

the anxiety, almost rage, of not being me
could harm the baby. But now it was late,

I couldn't be seen, and my mind
clattered and swarmed. What would I make

to eat that week, in Frost's kitchen?
Why hadn't I gone to Europe sooner,

worn hats, kept a place in New York?
Frost's children had eaten one-dish dinners

of boiled potatoes, and not from poverty.
Simplify, I said aloud, or you'll never be

consequential. Laughter from the yard.
I'd heard the joke before, semi-literary.

Out the window, stars caught in screens.
A single road lay ahead, open wide.

All I had to do was shoulder supplies.
All I had to do was provide.

Sage

Should I plant if what they say is true:
it delivers not only wisdom, but rescue
by eternal life? I'd prize its furry company
after everyone else was gone—family,
fellow readers, sworn companion—
and always be out of date, the only one,
crazy lady ringed by her favorite crop,
ladling beany soups from ancient pots,
recounting how a leaf outsmarted death.
Neighbor kids would flee, keen to accept
the course of things, suspecting thief or devil
in anything that sprang or seemed eternal.
Whoever approached, whoever fled the kitchen
wouldn't matter, nor whether it was written.

Adrienne Su is the author of three books of poems, Having None of It *(Manic D Press, 2009),* Sanctuary *(Manic D, 2006), and* Middle Kingdom *(Alice James Books, 1997). Her awards include a Pushcart Prize, an NEA fellowship, and a residency at The Frost Place in Franconia, NH. She teaches at Dickinson College in Pennsylvania, where she is poet-in-residence. Recent poems appear or are forthcoming in* The Kenyon Review, The New Republic, New England Review, *and* Southwest Review.

John Holman

The Burrison Prize

The Burrison Literary Prize luncheon was of interest to Ray for three reasons: He had begun a creative writing class on Tuesday nights and his teacher was a candidate for the prize; his friend Derek had surprised everyone by writing and publishing a novel that was also nominated this year; and it was a showcase for his serving business, Triangle Ray, that contracted to the hotel. Ray was managing the staff that would serve the hundred guests.

The cocktail reception was held in the lobby outside the doors of the hotel's Evergreen Room. Four of his bartenders took care of two bars at opposite ends of the room. Long tables against the middle wall held copies of the twelve nominated books, all vying to be named the year's best book of fiction by a North Carolina writer, as stipulated by the Burrison Literary Prize Committee and the writers they had hired to judge. Dressed-up people milled about, most sipping gin-and-tonics with lime, or chilled white wine, the pale gold color complementing the light spring hues of the women's silk and linen clothes. A few men wore blue or brown seersucker suits, solid knit ties or bright striped silks. Others wore blazers or Madras plaid jackets with ties. All were book club members and patrons of the arts taking the opportunity to hobnob with the artists. People who had time on a Thursday between 11 and 2 to get buzzed, have a meal, and listen to literary talk.

Ray looked around for Derek. His would be one the few dark faces among the guests, although a lot of people were already ostentatiously tanned for mid-April. Betty Daye, the Burrison Prize committee president, was one such person. She looked luxurious in a long, flowing dress of tiered shades of turquoise. She had her long frosted hair piled loosely atop her head, and moved quickly from task to task with bracelets of silver and large chunks of turquoise snicking along her gesturing wrists. A big blue-green spear of the stone stretched along the middle finger of her right hand, while a bright diamond sparked on her left. A few minutes ago, she had confirmed with Ray the number of vegetarian plates, and asked for a table on which to set the large, etched crystal bowl that would be given to the winner. Even her eyes were turquoise, with bursts of yellow surrounding the pupils. She was a beautiful old woman, the kind that fascinated Ray for her ability to overwhelm a person with graciousness while never allowing him to rally an equal response. Betty Daye was like a stage actress, with exaggerated manners that Ray would have felt like a fool trying to match. But such was the life of a servant in the South, Ray had observed. He could suppress his aversion and play the soft-spoken roles of minion and audience to the ruling exhibitionists.

While instructing Yusuf, a young waiter from UNC, to set up a table on the platform behind the lectern and to put a white cloth on it, Ray spotted his writing teacher, Abby Bishop, talking with a man who was almost as short as she was, and whose yellowish white hair was slicked back with deep comb tracks. Abby was drinking wine. A gold, emerald-eyed, spread-winged bug perched on a shoulder of her hot-pink jacket. This was funny, because in class she was against ornamentation and disdained self-consciousness. Ray was afraid of her, for unlike Betty Daye who made him feel inferior, Abby Bishop made him feel dumb. She gave back Ray's stories with adjectives, adverbs, and whole passages crossed out, and with marginal notes like "Muddy," "Huh?" and "What's at stake?" When she held forth about psychic distance, Ray wasn't sure what she meant.

But he went over to wish her good luck. "Hey, Teach," he said. "I hope you win."

"Hello, there, Fielding. You look sharp."

He wore the white waistcoat with the white shirt, black bowtie, black pants and shoes. "Thanks," he said. "You, too." He eyed the bug on her shoulder, a dragonfly, its four wings made of gold mesh, a tiny diamond at the tip of its tail. "That's quite a specimen."

"Meet my husband," she said. "He gave it to me. Putty, this is Ray Fielding, the waiter-slash-writer."

Putty nodded, shook hands. "I've heard about you folks. Abby needs to get over to the table and sign some books. Sounds like a funky class."

"Funky, funky," Ray said, snapping his fingers, bouncing a little. He felt nervous. It was always a little awkward running into people he knew from other areas of his life at work, even though he'd known Abby would be here today. But he'd never-ever pretended to be casual in her presence, and this was the place he should be most professional, the least casual. Or was it? This was his domain. Except his domain was always dominated by those he served.

"I teach Geology," Putty said, "so there's hardly any getting to know my students." His speech was slurred by a mouth that could only half-smile. A stroke mouth, probably.

"It's a class of nuts isn't it, Fielding?" Abby said. "Y'all excuse me to do my duty." She gave Putty her wine glass, mostly full, and scuttled off to the book table.

"Geology, huh?" Ray said.

"Yeah."

"Not entomology? The fancy bug and all."

"I should have given her a nice piece of gypsum?"

"It's a stunning insect. You made the better choice."

"Abby tells me you wrote a good story. She says you're one of her best."

"No kidding?" Ray looked at her back as she bent over the autograph table. She was a square-shaped woman, built like a box. "That's really sweet of her to say."

Putty slurped a laughed. "No, no. Abby is not sweet. If she said it, she meant it."

"Well, I'll tell you, that's more than flattering. It's flabbergasting."

"I'll tell her you said so."

"Oh, no. Please don't. But that's good news. I needed that."

"Who doesn't like praise?"

"I broke up with my girlfriend last night."

"So you did need it. It's not better than a girlfriend, though."

"I guess."

"Maybe you'll meet someone here. Life is full of the species, you know. Just look."

"Thanks, but I'm done for a while. Took forever to get out of that confusion."

"Yeah, it doesn't make sense, does it?"

"I wonder what Abby liked," Ray said, needing more.

"The three pigs, I think."

"Oh, cool. The fairy tale riff she asked us to do. Mine was about a home invasion. Did she tell you about the woman who reworked Snow White? Ms. White's being pimped by the dwarves? After the prince saves her, she plans to introduce him to Jesus, when they would live happily ever after."

Maybe that's what it took to be married to Abby Bishop, Ray thought. Drinks. Although sober, he too sort of loved her right then.

"The real Jesus?"

"That's what I wondered. Mixing up the fairy tales. Maybe just his ideas."

"Genre blending," Putty said.

Ray saw Derek enter the room. The cocktail crowd had thinned some as people wandered into the dining room to stake claims to tables. He could see his waiters pouring coffee for some of the guests. The water glasses had already been filled, ice already disappearing.

"Guess what," he said to Putty. "I'm working."

"See ya," Putty said. He looked at the wine glasses he held, one in each hand. "There's supposed to be a drunk writer or two at these things. I might give 'em some competition today."

Maybe that's what it took to be married to Abby Bishop, Ray thought. Drinks. Although sober, he too sort of loved her right then. He made it over to Derek who was talking to two women by the Evergreen Room entrance. They were beautiful women, young, neither one Derek's wife, who, Ray knew, wouldn't make it. She had to work, she said, when Ray called their house last night.

"This is Selma and this is Milla," Derek said, introducing them. "My buddy, Ray," he said to the women.

"Nice outfit," Selma said. She had a massive spray of curly, sand-colored hair.

Ray said, "I work here." He brushed the lapels of the waistcoat. "Are you up for the prize, too?" He wouldn't have been surprised if she were.

He knew to expect to be astonished by the young. Teenagers drove to the hotel in Aston Martins, Ferraris, and Bentleys, living lives full of confidence. With the band that entertained in the hotel lounge on weekends, a fourteen-year-old played guitar like Charlie Christian. Some of his college waiters seemed to know more about the wide world than he, at 42, did. These women looked to be in their twenties.

"We work with Derek at the paper," Selma replied. "He paid our way. And we like him."

"Groupies," Derek said.

"Yeah," said Selma.

The other woman, Milla, hadn't said anything, had barely looked at Ray, he noticed. She was the more alluring. She gazed out at the guests with startling dark-blue eyes. She had pale skin and a long nose, her straight dark hair in a low ponytail. "You're not from the United States, are you, Milla?" Ray asked.

"I'm from Europe," she said, turning to him, smiling, crossing one neat foot over the other and clasping her hands at her narrow waist. She wore a white blouse and a gray slender skirt. Her shoes were gray heels. "I was born in Bosnia, but I grew up in Germany." Not much of an accent. Her voice seemed to come from deeper inside her than most people's.

"Intern," said Derek. "Exchange student. Northwestern. My alma mater."

"Of course," Ray said. "I hope you like our modest America." Derek hadn't mentioned he'd bring company. Ray pointed Derek toward the book table. "You're supposed to sit over there and sign for whoever buys your novel."

There were name tags for the authors in front of folding chairs at the table. Abby Bishop sat at hers, now, but few of the others were claimed. Over the course of the reception, writers came and went from the table. At the moment, a tall man in a white Panama hat and a cinched black terry cloth bathrobe had the most attention. Under the robe showed a shirt and tie.

"Who's that?" Milla asked.

"The most assured," Derek said. "Bobby Router, author of *Socks*. It's about a half-breed, bi-sexual, schizophrenic."

"Autobiographical, I'll bet. He looks like a lot of things," Selma said.

"Not much time before lunch is served," Ray said. "You want to sit there for ten minutes? After that, you have to go in there and get the prize."

"Yeah, right. My little book about a child snail collector doesn't stand a chance against cornpone tomes about Great-grandma's sewing basket or magic mud pie."

"That's the one I want to read," Selma said. "I love magic food fiction."

"What's cornpone?" Milla asked.

"*Cone*pone," Derek said. "A genre of literature."

"Ever had mud pie?" Selma asked.

"No, not ever," Milla said.

"It's chocolate."

"I like chocolate."

"I have to check on some stuff," Ray said. "Good luck, man," he told Derek.

"Serve like the wind," Selma said.

The waiters knew their serving zones. The kitchen had rolled the warming carts containing the covered lunches to the side hallway. From the hall, three sets of double-doors led into the Evergreen Room, and all the staff had to do was load up two, three or four plates, depending on their skill, and place them in front of the guests. Two or three would work a table to get the food out fast, then separate for the rest of the meal to replenish drinks, one person to cover three tables of eight. For dessert, they'd regroup for fast clearing and serving. Ray would help out if he was needed, but mostly to show the others that he was a part of the team.

Authors' name tags were on the dining tables, too. Each table would seat at least one of the nominated writers, a souvenir memory for the non-writers who came for the $75 lunch. The guest speaker was seated at the front of the room near the raised podium, behind which now was a white cloth-covered table and the large crystal bowl. Ray strolled among the round banquet tables, checking again that everything looked right, and noting where Abby Bishop and Derek would sit.

Soon, Derek and his coworkers took their seats near the middle doors on the side of the room. White-haired women shared that table. Ray tried to take note of who the other nominees were, so few had manned the autograph table. He had recognized some famous names on the place tags. He figured the few men with beards, the black woman with cowry shells in her hair, and the heavy blonde guy in the wrinkled blue silk shirt were among the honored, as were a couple of thin white women with un-styled hair and in long lank skirts and flat shoes. If seating were any indication of rank, then Abby ranked high, her table with Putty directly behind that of Betty Daye and the guest speaker at the front.

The speaker's book was co-written with a more famous writer—a young white woman from the speaker's home state of Georgia. It had been widely praised. Ray had not read it, but it was supposed to be an unflinching portrait of poverty and illiteracy in the rural South. It chronicled the guest speaker's life of violence and deprivation, a life of cunning, compassion, and indomitable spirit. These were words in the brief biography printed on the luncheon's program. According to reviews, the man, a black man, Donny "Buck" Tate, had fathered eighteen children with various women, and had managed through many hardships—including prison and brain surgery—to find redemption through his late effort to claim and bring together his extended family. He and the co-writer, Tina Cockburn (pronounced Cokeburn), had appeared together on talk shows. Tina Cockburn wasn't here today. Donny "Buck" Tate had a large brown bald spot in the middle of his bushy, suspiciously black hair. Ray couldn't tell how old he was, but late 60's at least. He wore a brown suit with a yellow shirt. He sat quietly at his table, accompanied by Betty Daye and other Burrison Prize dignitaries, sipping iced tea.

While the plates were being served, Betty Daye stood at the lectern before the crystal bowl and explained the occasion. She told anecdotes about Dennis Burrison, the liberal newsman who, in the 60's, championed civil rights and mentored, she said, directly or indirectly, every major journalist in the South. She told of when she, herself, worked for him in his newsroom, of how he ruthlessly edited her work, sent her on assignments, and drank and flirted with her. "Dennis Burrison was a lover. A lover of people, of truth, and of language," she said. "But he would have been as astounded as proud that the prize for literature given in his name has held such prestige for now twenty-two years. The writers who have received it are among the best in the nation, let alone the South, and of course they represent the cream of our great state of North Carolina. This year's nominees are no less wonderful. They are sitting at your tables! Say hello to them!" People laughed, applauded, and nodded at their own personal authors. The authors nodded back, and Ray saw that he was right about some of his guesses.

As Betty Daye wrapped up her speech, instructing the diners to "Eat! Eat!," Ray slipped out to the lobby. Lunch and dessert would take about twenty or thirty minutes. Then Tate would speak. Then the judges would announce the winner. Everything should be completed in about an hour, an hour and a half. The bars would remain open. The bartenders, ever efficient, had already replenished ice, sliced limes, cherries, stirrers and napkins. One was reading *Entertainment Weekly*, another was hunched over a novel she must have borrowed from the book table. The room was empty of guests, and familiar sounds of cutlery on plates and the murmuring crowd issued mutedly through the closed Evergreen Room doors.

In the side hall, Ray checked the warming carts for leftover lunches. He lifted the silver top off one plate. A small quarter of broiled chicken, asparagus, and new potatoes. The vegetarian cart was empty, except for a round red-skinned potato that fell onto the speckled blue carpet. He picked it up. It was warm and moist, oily. His girlfriend, ex-girlfriend, now off-again-forever 35 year-old girlfriend, was vegetarian, and over three years had influenced his diet. They had finally ended it the day before over a dish of hummus and chickpeas at a party given by some of her library co-workers. No doubt that's why he was feeling adrift, along with having some time to kill before he had some work to do. Plus, he sort of wished he were a nominee for the Burrison prize. Usually, he felt no desire to be a part of the groups he served—the pharmaceutical people, the IT people, the wedding parties. Nobody here even knew he cared about writing except for Putty and Abby Bishop, and Derek. He went back to the lobby and threw the potato in the trash behind one of the bars. He didn't disturb the woman reading the novel. Instead, he chatted with the guy reading the entertainment magazine, got the scoop on upcoming movies and TV shows, until time for dessert. Then he washed his hands and went back inside to help serve.

Betty Daye got up again, this time to introduce the speaker. Through small, turquoise-rimmed glasses, she read from a sheet of paper, repeating what was printed on the program, and adding that "Mr. Donny Tate is a remarkable man, a special kind of genius of survival, a man who has pulled himself up from the absolute muck of life with his great determination to redeem and remake himself, and to forge healing bonds among his splintered, wounded family. As you all know, with the help of the esteemed Tina Cockburn, his life has been translated into a powerful and bold fictionalized memoir. I am so proud and pleased to have Mr. Tate here to share his hard earned wisdom with us." She extended her hands to him.

Tate practically leapt to the platform. He shook Betty Daye's jeweled hand and watched as she sat down. He smiled broadly, showing new teeth. He took a very deep breath before he said, "Call me Buck! My folks name me Donny. Some people wanna say Donald, but *that* not my name. Donny, after who I don't know. My friends call me Buck and I want everybody to be my friend. Buck, rhymes with…absolute muck! Ha! Luck, too. Gotta know that. *Everybody* is my friend, and *every day* is a good day." He looked around, grinning. He seemed nervous. His eyes, which were very light for such a dark man, goldish, seemed not to know where to settle.

"All right, now what? So much for the pree-ludes. I suppose y'all wanna know how I got eighteen childrens. That what Oprah wanted to know, too. I said, How do you think, Oprah? Did y'all see that? She asked me if I knew about birth's control. When I was a boy, we didn't know hardly nothing but what we likeded and didn't like. Them little girls I was messing with then, they just took to me, that's all. And I likeded them, too. Also the grown womens, you know, then and later. They likeded my eyes, they say. I got these white eyes." He widened them. "Which, by the way, I like your eyes, too, Miss Betty Daye. Like sunrise. Ha!"

Betty Daye drew back. Ray couldn't see her face, but he imagined her looking shocked and amused. Because she probably was. And she had her table to entertain.

"That how everything got started," Buck Tate said, "with me liking too much, being likeded back, and not knowing what was wrong with it. You wouldn't know anything was wrong with it, would you? But there's plenty. I went to jail. First for not paying support. Then for stealing to pay support. Other things led on from that. They tried to get me for statuary rape. Turns out, everybody wasn't none of my friend! I been shot, stabbed, beat up, lied about, operated on. I still has a bad psychotic nerve, comes and goes.

"I suppose y'all wanna know how I got eighteen childrens. That what Oprah wanted to know, too. I said, How do you think, Oprah? Did y'all see that? She asked me if I knew about birth's control."

Makes my leg hurt so I limp sometime. I feels good today. Oh, and I likeded mens, too, and vicey-versy.

"But I never did like childrens. I like babies, though. When I was in grade school, childrens picked at me, called me 'punk' and the like. I got beat up. I don't like childrens 'cause you can't trust 'em. Even my grandchildrens. I used to wear vanilla flavoring on my skin, see. I likeded my hair and skin shining. Shiny long fingernails. I used to wear my pants a certain way, low on my hips so my hips could sway. I told everything to Miss Tina and she wrote it all down. But like I told Larry Kang on "The Larry Kang Show," I have finally *almost* had enough of woman stuff now. And I don't wont nothing up the butt, neither!"

When parts of the crowd laughed (Ray heard Derek practically shriek), Tate stopped and looked baffled and surprised. But still smiling, he looked up at the ceiling, at the huge cystal chandeliers hanging in the space above the crowd like inverted twinkling trees. He chuckled. He said, "It sparkly in here."

Ray noticed Yusuf, the kid who'd helped with the podium table, standing along the far wall, poker-faced. All the serving staff, most of them black, just stood, having stopped pouring water, tea, and coffee for the speech. Yusuf held his chin high. Ray wondered what effect Tate's talk was having on him and the others.

"I'm dressed up now," Tate said, "but one time I was the dirtiest man you ever saw. I did all kinds of down on the ground work. I did yard work where about I loaded up a lawnmower with rakes and clippers and pushed 'em up the roads looking for work. I might get a few dollars to eat with but my shack didn't have 'lectric and I just wore what I worked in all the time. When it were cold, I stayed in a mission for mens. Bad days, let me say. No mens or womens likes a dirty man."

Ray left the room then, astonished

Maybe Betty Daye hadn't stolen anything. Tate didn't seem to care about his dignity; if he had any, he'd given it away. But Betty Daye had definitely used him. She knew the man would look like a fool. And she enjoyed it.

by Donny Tate's ignorance, his incoherence, his total lack of preparedness for such a gathering. It was embarrassing. He was furious with Betty Daye. She had invited Tate instead of Cockburn, the real writer. But both of those women had exploited Tate. One took his story, and the other stole—what? Maybe Betty Daye hadn't stolen anything. Tate didn't seem to care about his dignity; if he had any, he'd given it away. But Betty Daye had definitely used him. She knew the man would look like a fool. And she enjoyed it. And where was Cockburn now?

A voice behind him said, "How do you like old Trueblood in there?"

Ray turned to see Selma and Milla. It was Selma who had spoken, her accent pure piedmont. A few other people had come out too, headed for the bars.

"He's hard to believe," Ray said. "Not that I'm saying he's a liar."

"He's quite a character," Milla said.

Ray laughed. "Can I get you a drink?" he asked.

"Do you have beer?" asked Milla.

Selma held up two fingers. "This many," she said.

Ray went behind a bar and grabbed three iced bottles from the tub there. "I shouldn't drink here," Ray said. He had a small office he could invite them to. It was too small. "Want a tour of the kitchen?" he asked.

"Not really," Selma said. She reached in the pocket of her dress for a tissue, which she wrapped around the wet bottle. The dress was pale green. The pockets had white daisies with yellow centers embroidered along the openings, and the same pattern traced the scoop of the dress's neck.

"Sorry. You want a napkin?" he asked Milla.

She shook her head, looking at him sideways, the bottle already upturned to her lips.

Selma said. "Let's go to my car. Listen to some tunes. Drink in peace."

Ray led them out a side door and around to the front of the building. Selma's car was an old red two-door Civic. Ray sat in the back, his knees against the passenger seat where Milla sat. Selma turned on a Stevie Wonder CD. "Is this where Derek sits?" he asked.

"We be chauffeurs," Selma said.

Milla's sleek, straight ponytail was hidden by the headrest, and Selma's crinkly hair, which spread across her back and shoulders, was held away from her face by daisy clips at the temples. Selma clinked her bottle against

Milla's, and then both women turned to share the toast with Ray. "To lunch," Selma said. Ray swallowed about half his beer. Selma lit a joint with the lighter from the dashboard. The smell brought on instant nostalgia. She passed the joint to Milla, who daintily drew on it. Selma said, "The Burrison Prize is a freak show."

Ray didn't answer. He let Stevie Wonder fill the silence. He wondered what Milla knew of race subtleties in America. He knew too little about the ethnic conflicts in Bosnia, and of Germany he knew only about the WWII troubles of Jews, neither of which seemed subtle. He said, "Well, you know, it's disappointing. That's all I can say."

"Here," Milla said, giving him the joint. It was rolled with brown paper. Stevie Wonder was singing "All Is Fair in Love," and as the pot took effect, his sense of nostalgia deepened. He hadn't smoked since college, when that song was soothing after his marriage ended. He'd gotten married just out of high school, and it lasted two years. Now, thinking about breaking up with his girlfriend yesterday, and feeling the sad euphoria of long ago, he felt in two eras at once, like two people, even. He could see himself in the backseat of some car outside the country club where he used to work, getting high with some of his co-workers then, letting the smoke lighten his mood about his wife's unhappiness. Yet here he was now with two strange young women, trying to lighten his mood about the day before, about Buck Tate and Betty Daye, about tomorrow being empty of purpose.

He passed the joint to Selma. Suddenly he wasn't sure what race she was. He had thought she was a white woman. Not just her light skin, but the daisies as well suggested that to him. She had blue eyes, but Buck Tate had light eyes. Her nose was sort of blunt but small, and her lips were sort of full and pouty, and her hair was thick. Of course she was white, he thought, and why should he care? He didn't. But he wanted to know, and he didn't know how to ask.

Then he said, "Are you white?"

Both Selma and Milla turned around.

"Dude," Selma said. "Are you high?"

"Is Selma your real name?"

She squinted as she pulled on the joint. "No, it's Aleve," she said, exhaling. "And Milla is actually Nuprin. You got a pain and we can soothe it. Derek tells me you got dumped last night. You want us to take the hurt away?"

"You're doing it. And it was a co-dump situation. We were a dead couple walking. Still, thanks for being medicine. Otherwise, Derek talks too much."

"He's good gossip. That's why we like Derek."

"I like him, too," Ray said.

"And you married young."

"Yeah. So? He told you a lot."

"That's sort of interesting. Makes you kind of romantic."

"He never said a word about you."

"We're secrets. What happened last night?"

"Nothing. I don't know. Time. Used to be, I was so infatuated that I'd drive by where she lived just to see it, hoping she might be in the yard. For months she played like merely a friend, always side-stepping my little love talk. By the time she figured she could like me for real, I was pretty much over it. But I pretended I wasn't."

By the time she figured she could like me for real, I was pretty much over it.

"Then, months later, you resented her. And she started hating you for it."

"I don't know. I guess. Ask Derek."

"Hey, did you see Donny Tate hit on the lady that introduced him? He's *almost* given up woman stuff. Milla and I might have to meet Buck Tate ourselves."

"Are you sure you're white? Mixed, maybe?" Ray asked.

"Are we not all? It's a mixed up shook up world. Just ask the guy in the bathrobe. Right, Milla?"

"I'm neutral," Milla said, tight-voiced, before exhaling a conical cloud. She coughed.

"Look at me, sitting here getting stoned with race-neutral women."

"You put a word in my mouth," Milla said. She gave him back the joint, which was getting too short.

Ray squeezed in some smoke. He listened to Stevie Wonder. He shifted his weight so that he leaned against the door behind Milla, his legs angled across the backseat. He said, "When I was a kid, I didn't know there were different kinds of white people. Then it turned out there were Jewish white people and Italian white people and Hungarians. Nowadays, there are different kinds of black people, too. First, there's all non-white people. Then, you have your Caribbean black people, your African black people, your Jewish black people, your Hispanic black people. I used to think people from India, with straight hair, were a special kind of black people, but I don't think that's what they think they are. That's when I was a kid and there'd be photos of dark, glossy-haired families on these religious brochures at church. Maybe they were Sri Lankan families. Anyway, I had a waiter once, a student who was born in Korea, but adopted and raised by a white family in Maryland. She was just starting to identify as Asian. She invited me to the Korean Student's Association dinner at the university. They offered Korean food and cultural entertainment, you know, a demonstration of Korean martial arts. But then a group of boys came out and did some break dancing. Next, Korean music videos featuring a blinged-out, dyed-blonde dude hip-hopping brag-rap, all swinging gold chains and sideways cap. So mixed up is definitely the thing. But leave it to Betty Daye and Buck Tate to bring back the good old pure American dichotomy and cringe."

"Wow," said Selma.

"I'm putting this out," Ray said.

"Throw it out the window."

Ray doused the joint with wet fingertips and put it in his pants pocket. "Keepsake," he said, although neither woman was looking back at him.

Milla said, "I can see the fascination with Buck Tate. I'd like to read his book. Properly organized, his story could be compelling."

"Tina Cockburn thought so," Ray said.

"I like the way he sounds," Milla continued. "Like a cross between a bulldog and melting chocolate ice cream."

"Gee," said Selma, "I want to hear that."

"Didn't you?" Milla said.

Selma said, "He sounded to me like a soft pulpy log and Juicy Fruit chewing gum."

They started laughing. Ray did too. He tried to think of what Tate sounded like to him, and it was on the tip of his tongue, but the thought of that, that phrase, plus what Milla and Selma had said, made him unable to stop laughing. Tate kind of looked like a log, and a bulldog, thick and short, and the furrows in his forehead were like chewed gum, and his words melted together, and he sounded just like he looked. Ray's stomach muscles hurt, tears blurred his vision, and the women's laughter was the same high pitch of Stevie Wonder's harmonica, which was playing *Boogie On Reggae Woman* now.

"I gots to go hear that guy again," Selma said.

"I gots to too," Milla said. They convulsed in hilarity again. They opened the car doors, let Ray out the backseat, and all three brushed ash off their clothes, laughing. Ray felt guilty for laughing at Buck. Then he realized that he was probably in a paranoid haze. "He has a head like an amphitheater," Ray said.

"A coliseum," Milla said.

"A racetrack," Selma said.

"Whew!" Ray said. He was glad that all he'd have to do soon was break down the room—clear the tables and gather the tablecloths—a fairly mindless activity that being stoned should make pleasant and light.

When they got back to the Evergreen Room they heard applause from outside the closed doors. Good, Ray thought, Donny "Buck" Tate was done. The applause, though, was for the names of the nominated writers, which were being recited by one of the old men he'd seen wearing blue seersucker. He had a white handkerchief fluffed out of his jacket pocket. He had a droopy, jowly face with a pouch of folds under his chin, pouchy eyes, and a high, wavy white pompadour hairstyle, so that he looked like a cone of vanilla soft-serve. Ray turned to suggest that to Selma and Milla, but they were making their way down the side aisle toward the table they shared with Derek.

In his story, the guy would have just broken up with his longtime girlfriend, and would have sworn off women for a while, but these two women would be so much fun and so pretty that he'd want to fall in love with them both. He'd want them [...]

Soon, the man got to Derek's name. Derek stood, as the others had done, and turned about and waved at the audience. Ray raised his arm from the back, feeling proud that his buddy was in this mix. One day, Ray thought, he too might be seated in the audience, a fêted nominee. Maybe he could write a story about a guy meeting two beautiful women who get him high.

They'd be at a party maybe, sitting on pillows with tiny mirrors sewn into the fabric. That's what the pillows were like at the party last night. In his story, the guy would have just broken up with his longtime girlfriend, and would have sworn off women for a while, but these two women would be so much fun and so pretty that he'd want to fall in love with them both. He'd want them, or just one, to fall for him. Yet he wouldn't know what to say or do to manage it, because....

The ice cream man now named the winner of the Burrison Prize. "For a book of profound emotion, compassion and human truth, composed of heartbreaking beauty, a book that practically emits sparks from every page, this year's Burrison Prize goes to Imogine Cameron, the author of *Churn*.

During the cheers and applause, a woman made her way from the middle of the room to the lectern, where she accepted the crystal bowl and a check. She stood for a moment not saying a word, just looking at the bowl. Then into the microphone she said, "Thank you," in a voice so flat and country is seemed a put-on. Her hair was long and black, curled about her shoulders like Loretta Lynn's, or some other old-fashioned country singer, and her dress was just a long drape of navy cloth. She held the bowl under one arm like a giant football. "I just want to say that this is an honor I will never forget, that I never dared to dream of. And believe me, I dream all the time." Chuckles scattered through the audience. "My book is about the kind of people I know, mountain

He wanted to kiss her, as if he would taste the sound. He wanted to kiss Milla, too, who sounded, he decided, like a clarinet. And Selma, whose lips were plump and red, whose tongue was tart.

people that always fascinated me for their courage and foolishness, their fight, you know. I couldn't have thought you'd think so much of them."

As she continued, Ray was taken by the spell of her voice. He wanted to get closer, to see better the movement of her lips, the lift of her tongue, but he didn't leave his station at the back of the room. From there, he could see that her lips were thin and pink. They produced a sound he didn't know that real people made. It was beautiful and—what? Beguiling. He wanted to kiss her, as if he would taste the sound. He wanted to kiss Milla, too, who sounded, he decided, like a clarinet. And Selma, whose lips were plump and red, whose tongue was tart. He wanted them to pass their speech to him that way, kissing, kissing, kissing. He thought of Abby Bishop. He didn't want to kiss her, and shuddered to imagine it, but he did want to cast a similar spell for her. She'd tell Putty, over wine they shared in their comfortable living room, surfaces decorated with fossils and sparkly stones from Putty's geological expeditions, "You remember Ray Fielding, the waiter-slash-writer? I love that guy. I love that guy so much."

John Holman is the author of a short story collection, Squabble and Other Stories, *and a novel,* Luminous Mysteries. *His stories also have appeared in such publications as* The New Yorker, Mississippi Review, Crescent Review, Apalachee Quarterly, Carolina Quarterly, Oxford American, *and* Alabama Literary Review. *His work has also appeared in various anthologies. Holman has received grants and awards for his writing from the Winston-Salem Arts Council, the North Carolina Cultural Arts Coalition, the University of South Florida Research and Creative Scholarship Fund, and the Mrs. Giles Whiting Foundation.*

Billy Collins

The Juice Glass

One of the more memorable questions that came up
that morning as I lay on a white couch
in a summer cottage set back from the beach
contemplating a juice glass
encircled with multi-colored stripes,

was what size vessel it would take
to contain all the tears shed in a lifetime.

Two dogs were barking next door,
small dogs by the sound of their pipsqueak barking,
and a fishing smack was chugging along
just under the horizon, left to right,
which I read as I would read a line of type.

Then I went to the sink to fill
the colorful juice glass with water to the brim
and set it on the counter next to the silvery toaster,

and that is just how you found me
as you emerged sleepily from the bedroom—
staring at the collected tears of a girl
who had died quite young
or of an old man who had rarely cried.

What a way for a day to begin, I thought—
your warm arms around me, head tilted on my chest
as I lifted the glass and drank it all down, eyelash and all.

A Restaurant in Moscow

Even here among the overwhelming millions
and the audible tremble of history,
a solemn trout stared up at me
as it lay on its side on a heavy white plate
next to some broccoli and shards of broken bread.

I could tell from its expression,
or lack of expression, that is was pretending
not to listen to my silent questions about its previous life—
its cold-water adventures, its capable mother—
and that its winking at me was a trick of candlelight.

But soon, all that was left
was the spine and a filigree of bones,
so I sat back to finish off the wine
and drink in this place that had comforted me
with its chests of ice where fish were bedded,

drawings of fish in frames on the white walls,
and the low music. Backed by a hint
of guitar sang a broken-hearted woman
I imagined to be my waitress
who had no English, nor I any Russian,

and who never once smiled, yet she had waited
for me to close my notebook
and put away my pen before clearing my plate
as if she understood the provocative nature of this trout.
And how sweet to realize this only later

after I had put on my raincoat
and was back in the drizzle of the wide boulevard
among pedestrians on their private missions,
heading downhill back to my hotel
with St. Basil's colorful domes lit up in the misty distance.

Billy Collins has published ten collections of poetry, including Questions About Angels, The Art of Drowning, Sailing Alone Around the Room: New & Selected Poems, Nine Horses, The Trouble With Poetry and Other Poems, Ballistics, Horoscopes for the Dead *and* Picnic, Lightning. *He has edited two anthologies of contemporary poetry:* Poetry 180: A Turning Back to Poetry *and* 180 More: Extraordinary Poems for Every Day. *He was the guest editor of* The Best American Poetry 2006. *Collins has received fellowships from the New York Foundation for the Arts, the National Endowment for the Arts, and the Guggenheim Foundation.*

Naomi Shihab Nye

Conundrum

My Jewish friends are kind and gentle.
Not one of them would harm another person
even if they didn't know that person.
I would bet on this.

My Arab friends are kind and gentle.
Not one of them would harm another person
even if they didn't know that person.
I would bet on this.
They might press you to drink 45 small cups
of coffee or tea but that would be the extent of it.

My Jewish friends have never taken my house,
my land, pressed me into a small cell, tortured me,
killed my parents, insulted my existence,
never once, not at all. If I have a tree, they admire it.
They don't cut it down. Their ancestors
may have done that to mine and my ancestors
may never have recovered, but we are new people
now, and should behave as such.

They respect me as an equal.
I have never said they should not exist.
They have never tried to erase me.

Naomi Shihab Nye's most recent book is The Turtle of Oman *(Greenwillow, 2014)—a chapter book for children.*

Wyn Cooper

The Loneliest Road in America

—for Laure-Anne Bosselaar

A long crooked line   across Nevada   US 50
alone with bright thoughts   and big sky
east to west   from Baker to Reno
400 miles   over 12 mountain ranges
a rare smile   large as the land

Dusk is the hour   between dog and wolf
howling and howling   where is my darling
why am I on this road   so straight and stark
everything I'm not   this isn't about you
or me   or anyone   who hasn't traveled this road

Hallucinations ensue   as the sun descends
I drive into the sunset   of course I do
but this time alone   so what's the point
except for the green ray   I see when the sun
drops below the horizon   tripping on light

Stars are my guide   as I glow and glide
across miles of pavement   listening hard
celestial music   I sing along to
the tires a sound   I can't block out
until one of them blows   middle of nowhere

I find a bright red shirt   on the shoulder
to wave at passing cars   but there are no cars
I need no help   I wave it instead
at all the people   not alive anymore
just short epitaphs   in the graveyard here

Intense

Intense is an
intriguing word:
could mean strong,
severe, extreme; could
mean in actual tents,
could mean homicides
gone terribly
awry, getaway
cars out of gas,
the pale drivers
slumped over their
steering wheels, dead
of exhaust fumes.

We live in a tent
and it's intense,
the winter colder
than falling snow
which covers our tent,
then warms it until
it caves in on us,
the last straw,
the silver dollar
no one wants,
the albino deer
dead on the trail.

Gunfire

Gunfire in the night wakes me
in bed: I cower under covers.
The last shot comes through the wall
just under your photo, framed
in gilt, your smile disarming,
flight in your eyes. The bullet
hole lets winter air blow into
the room, a chill I know too well.

At dawn the hunters return to gather
their kill, drag it slowly back
to their truck in my driveway,
speed away with Thrill Kill Kult
blasting at full volume, the name
of their state on their license plate,
numbers that add up to eleven,
number of days since you went away.

Wyn Cooper's fourth book of poems, Chaos Is the New Calm, *was published by BOA Editions in 2010. His poems appear in 25 anthologies of contemporary poetry and more than 100 magazines, including* Poetry, The Southern Review, *and* Slate. *He has taught at Bennington and Marlboro Colleges, the University of Massachusetts/Amherst, the Frost Place, and at the University of Utah. He has written songs with Sheryl Crow, David Broza, Jody Redhage, and David Baerwald. Songs from his two CDs with Madison Smartt Bell can be heard on six television shows. He lives in Vermont and recently worked for the Harriet Monroe Poetry Institute, a think tank run by the Poetry Foundation in Chicago. He currently works as a freelance editor of poetry, fiction, and non-fiction.* www.wyncooper.com

Bruce Weigl

Against Forgetting (one)

Startling, when the brain can see the mind;
accomplished only with the most precise
surgery for example, performed by beings
whose hands are made of a kind of glass
that you are not allowed to touch.
They only fit inside of you.
You are not allowed to ask
certain questions afterwards;
questions about the paradigm
are especially discouraged,
and never appreciated.
They maintain security at all times.
I want to ask if I am the same, or different,
but it is not allowed, and even before the thought
completes itself, and the words are not yet on my lips,
someone is tsking to me inside of my head,
wagging their finger like a mother or a drug cop
in the rearview mirror of my horizon.
One misstep in this situation could bring trouble,
ask just about any dead soul still spinning around
in circles, wondering, What the fuck was that?

Bruce Weigl is the author of thirteen collections of poetry, most recently The Abundance of Nothing, *a finalist for the Pulitzer Prize in Poetry for 2012. His poetry, translations, essays and reviews have appeared widely and in such forums as* The New York Times, The New Yorker, The Paris Review, Harpers, The American Poetry Review, *For his work he has been awarded the Pushcart Prize twice, an award from the Academy of American Poets, a Breadloaf and Yaddo Foundation Fellowship, a National Endowment for the Arts grant in poetry, The Cleveland Arts Prize, the Ohioana Poetry Prize, an award for "contributions to American Culture" from the Vietnam Veterans of America, The Robert Creeley Award for Poetry, and a Lannan Foundation Award in Poetry.*

Kate Johnson

Late Fall

Certain days, late fall, mid-February, when I consider killing myself, I think about the dog. Who's going to feed him, sit in the grass and explain, in the mist of dandelion weed, that dying doesn't mean not loving? Oh dog, some people will try to sail all kinds of nonsense by you when they're afraid of their own feelings. No, I can't leave it to a stranger to rub your sunlit belly till one hind leg twitches in the air.

If anyone's going to lie to the dog, I should because he trusts me the most, which makes as much sense as children walking to Sunday School, shiny bright, their best pastels. When a deep trust is broken, nothing seems real again. No spring or summer returns to the splintered self…. And shit, even if I did kill myself, how could I? I mean he's licking his toenails and now my face.

Peonies

God, on whom I have just slammed
my shabby door. God of the crimson

azaleas, god of light and untried
crimes, unspeakable

god of love—today the peonies open
to ants darting across their sugary heads. Ruby

pink, stems the green of wind, but tall-headed,
listing now. Each

needs to be held, loosely bound
and staked. Do you think, dear

god, that this is a poem
about peonies?

Kate Johnson is the author of three collections of poetry including When Orchids Were Flowers, This Perfect Life, *and* Wind Somewhere, and Shade. *She teaches in the creative writing program at Sarah Lawrence College.*

Ron Smith

The Birth of Modern Poetry

Chucked out of the Academy,
          he sails straight
     to a pastry shop
              where the darkness laps
        the gossip in his head,
the whispers. That line
      lashed to that gondola:
             how it goes slack, goes taut.
"Suffering

        exists in order
           to make people think,"
     he will tell the daughter
        he can't yet imagine and certainly
does not want. Does he know
          what he wants? A good pasta and something
    potable. Liquid darkness and sputtering tapers—
           flickers—but, sometimes
               hard as gems…

You can spend an evening
          in the mask shop
    filling in
those empty eyes. Who really cares
          if he sinks or swims? Homer

       and Isabel. Hilda and Bill. He eats, when he eats,
too fast. The knife's silver edge: the grinding: that Yeats
        he reads and reads: he'll get

to goddamn London and change the world.
        Which way to change it? How do you know?
    You make it new, make it up as you go,
                and you keep on moving.

Just the Big Three

I.

Shower, I'm alone in the team shower.
Steam and silence.

The locker room is empty. I am dream
dressing. Music. In the gym?

Petula Clark is downtown.
I emerge into darkness blurring
with music and people dancing.

Oh, yeah, the sock hop.
I don't remember anything else.

Somebody told me I couldn't
get my shoulder pads off,

that Coach cut them off with scissors.

II.

That's my friend's face, what's
his name, laughing at me, he
looks so happy. Bobby, he says.
I'm Bobby? And he nearly goes
down laughing. *My girlfriend's
name is Bert?* Oh, my God,
he says, electric glee all over him.

I do know one thing, I say, and
now I'm laughing, too. *I weigh
one hundred and ninety-four pounds.*

They sent me to a doctor that time,
the *only* time in ten years—they sent
me to the local quack, the one who
had sewed a small turd of mud
into my ripped calf two years before.
They say I smiled all day, went
to bed chuckling.

III.

Again, hilarity, my friend in the helmet,
Jim, yes, Jim, All-American receiver, such
snickering and hooting and he says
we're both here on the bench, because.

We're way down the bench, away
from the coaches.

                     Later, they tell me
I was grinning when they leaned down
to lift me. I was snuggling
the fifty yard line, the grass and the chalk.

Every other time, I was walking around,
zombie style, upright. That was the *only* time,
I swear, that I was down and out.
Jesus. Karsarda said I had gone
for the kicker's knee just as he lifted it,
hard. *Did* he *go down?* Oh, hell, yeah, he said,
but he got right up.

Barelli Calls

When it rings, the phone
                    I forgot to turn off, I might
as well answer it—that delicate
                    metaphor, that gauzy scrim
of innuendo that married the world
          to the spirit yet somehow kept them
separate, that draped the one in the merely
                              glittering other—
                    it's gone.

Yo, Smitty, I hear you got a book coming out.
I can feel that forearm. Blocking Barelli
was like blocking a tree trunk or an anvil.
My neck begins to ache. God, it's great
to hear that mob movie accent I haven't
heard in years. Barelli, next to me on the bus
from the Hattisburg airport to the hotel:
Smitty, what's that fucking stuff in the trees?
You're kidding, right? But Barelli's cartoon
consternation's perfectly genuine. *Spanish*
moss? Jesus, that's gross!

                    Today, he claims
to remember a pig on a porch outside the airport
but doesn't remember when I asked him about
pickpockets in the Bronx. *Pickpockets?* he said.
No, Smitty. Guys just hit you over the head
with a pipe and take their time. Pickpockets?
That's British, I think.

A surgeon wanted to cut
his shoulder. *Tell me, Doc,* he said, *if this was your
shoulder, would you do that? No, Doc, that hesitation's
just a little too long, thanks. Smitty, I could have
thrown the guy up the wall, so, yeah, I'm OK
after all these years, no complaints.*

We talk for hours, Delores looking in
from time to time, whispering Dinner?

*...So, I wanted to tell ya, I'm bodyguarding
Ted Williams, you know, before he got sick,
and we're sitting there at lunch and he's such
a nice guy, always a gentleman with me and
his son's right there and I say, You know, Ted,
it's amazing, he looks just like you. And
Ted leans back and says, Yeah, but he can't
play baseball for shit.*

Ron Smith, the Poet Laureate of Virginia is the author of the books Its Ghostly Workshop, Moon
Road: Poems 1986-2005, *and* Running Again in Hollywood Cemetery *(1988). Running Again
in Hollywood Cemetery was judged by Margaret Atwood "a close runner-up" for the National Poetry
Series Open Competition and was subsequently published by University Presses of Florida.* Moon Road
and Its Ghostly Workshop *were published by LSU Press. Smith's books have been highly praised by
reviewers and by distinguished writers. Ron Smith's work has appeared in numerous periodicals, including*
The Nation, Southern Review, Kenyon Review, Virginia Quarterly Review, Georgia Review,
Shenandoah, Kansas Quarterly, Blackbird, Puerto del Sol, *and* Verse. *His poems have also
appeared in a number of anthologies published in the United States, Canada, Great Britain, and Italy.*

Tim Seibles

Amnesia Villanelle

Seems ta seem, lately, like I'm turning sorta numb
The records in my head been double-stacked with dust
Wish someone could tell me where the blues came from

Been listening to black radio   and honestly, I'm stunned
That one door to my heart is almost black with rust
I'm starting to believe I must be halfway numb

Why you think this question won't stop pullin on my thumb?
Pretty soon or later   I think my head might bust
Wonder where the hell and gone these heavy blues came from

Betcha Bessie Smith would know, but she ain't gonna come
People steady scold me: *Why you gotta make a fuss?*
I can tell they're thinkin *Gotdamn, this dude is dumb!*

I guess there's old man Clapton—and long gone Stevie Vaughn
You know *I* know forgetting   has been a useful crutch
Maybe *you* could call me   whisper where the blues is from

I walk some blues and concentrate; it doesn't help to run
But this big hole in memory sorta makes it kinda rough
Jus hold my hand and tell me, dollins, you don't think I'm dumb
Can anyone remember where the fuck these blues came from?

Bizzy Blues Villanelle

I chase my life, but my life gets away
My mental hinge is sittin pretty loose
Heavy Monday   runs down the day

I warn my beard, but it still turns gray
Kiss the *Coppertop* tryin to steal some juice
I plead my case, but my life's in the way

Why move my mouth if my mouth can't say?
The soul calls me home, but I remain aloof
Bizzy Tuesday burns down the day

You gotta wonder who filleted this fillet
Got a bone in my throat almost thick as a spruce
I hold onto my life; then my life goes astray

I'm back on my back like my bug's been sprayed
Whose funky chickens have come home to roost?
Another run   undoes the day

If gospel was gospel I just might pray
Them green eggs and ham didn't save Dr. Seuss
I rub the lamp   but the genie walks away

You tune up your car, but that car won't play
Smoke some herb so your heart can get loose
Bizzy Wednesday breaks down the day

They tell me I'm lucky—it don't feel that way
Seems like I'm the black cat on a hot tin roof

I plead with myself, but my self won't stay
Always bizzy: another day re-does the day

A Piacere: Iago, Unfettered

I'm no green
monster: I've shared
my share of sweat-
damp sheets—and with maidens
deadly more fair
than Desdemona, I dare say.

What *is* romance? A two-faced
beast, each saying always
what the other
misunderstands. Such fuss
finds web for silly flies.
Tis trouble

that I love, its inscrutable
stealth: the way it
appears from nowhere
and gains all
attention—like an unfathered
birth   or a bad ghost
who spurs your head
till you give up the lease
and go.

Comfort comes in believing
men could not be cruel
but for ignorance
of kinder ways. *Romance*
indeed! Yet the lack

of such faith cuts and bleeds
unbearable days, while
an abundance of it threads
mischief into lovely lives: lo,
I did not do what I did
for meanness sake. Othello,

don't claw your face. Regret
is a legless steed. I confess
I found you marvelous: a heart
more stout than most—
with a head to match—but
such a riddle   then

what mortal fun: to build
a weather brash and black
enough to blow you down
and snuff love's lamp
in the same now.

To see it *done*   and live
to hear that sharp
consumptive cry. O, more
than this, I could not hope
to ask.

Tim Seibles is the author of several poetry collections including Hurdy-Gurdy, Hammerlock, *and* Buffalo Head Solos. *His first book,* Body Moves, *(1988) has just been re-released by Carnegie Mellon U. Press as part of their Contemporary Classics series. His latest,* Fast Animal, *was one of five poetry finalists for the 2012 National Book Award. In 2013 he received the Pen Oakland Josephine Miles Award for poetry and received an honorary Doctorate of Humane Letters from Misericordia University for his literary accomplishments. Most recently, he received the Theodore Roethke Memorial Poetry Award for* Fast Animal, *given triennially for a collection of poems.*

He has been a workshop leader for Cave Canem, a writer's retreat for African American poets, and for the Hurston/Wright Foundation, another organization dedicated to developing black writers. Tim is visiting faculty at the Stonecoast MFA in Writing Program sponsored by the University of Southern Maine. He lives in Norfolk, Virginia, where he is a member of the English and MFA in writing faculty at Old Dominion University.

Richard Blanco

Genius of Stars and Love

On the occasion of The Tech Awards,
The Tech Museum of Innovation,
San Jose California, November 2013

The tiny billion eyes of the stars have seen it all.
They've watched us as long as we've stared up
at them, their twinkle whispering in our eyes, eons
before our tongues tamed breaths into words
that could name them, chart and connect them
in the likeness of our heroes, gods, and beasts.
They knew our minds would dare kindle fire: fire
to cook, to draw and write with soot, fire to reach
the moon someday, then aim toward their sparkle.
They knew once they heard the first tree we felled
and hollowed into a hull, cutting across the mirror
of a lake to a far shore—simply because there was
a farther shore. They held our hands stitching sails
to cup wind across seas, glide over the flat earth
before it was round to us. They knew, following us
as we followed them for centuries to map our world
in pastel colors, then stitch continents with tracks,
roads veining over the land. They knew we'd solve
the mystery of bones and feathers to forge steel
into wings for ourselves, kiln sand into glass to peer
at our cells dividing, atoms spinning, and the heart
of their starriness breathing like our own bodies.
They saw us speak with smoke, then dots-dashes—
now they eavesdrop on our voices, pixels made air
traveling at the speed of light through our satellites

like fireflies flashing beside them in the night sky. Sky
from which they've also mourned our wars, pitied
our crisp air turned heavy and dark, our reflections
drowned in rivers and lakes spoiled by our spoils,
our land stripped barren by drought and flood.
They knew. But they waited, hoping someday
we'd understand what we're understanding now:
it takes the soul's mind as much as the gears
of love if we are to survive ourselves and reach
their starlight someday. Love to graph the arc
of a child's smile tasting fresh water, tasting
a fresh tomorrow. Love to design an arm of steel
for an armless man, measure the joy in his eyes
able to touch his wife's face. Love to calculate
what we took, must return to the earth to sow
the seeds of a farmer's trust. Love to integrate
all the voices of the voiceless into the gigabytes
of words claiming the world. Love to harness
light to give life and save lives, the same light
from the stars that have always known: love
is our wisest formula, most elegant calculation,
our most noble science, most brilliant invention.
Love, our greatest genius, as genius as the fire
in the still eyes of the stars, still watching us.

Richard Blanco is the author of City of a Hundred Fires *(1998),* Directions to the Beach of
the Dead *(2005),* Looking for the Gulf Motel *(2012),* One Today *(2013),* Boston Strong
(2013), and For All of Us, One Today: An Inaugural Poet's Journey *(2013). In 2013, Blanco
was chosen to serve as the fifth inaugural poet of the United States, becoming the youngest, first Latino,
immigrant and openly gay writer to hold the honor. His poems have appeared in countless literary journals
and anthologies, including* Best American Prose Poems *and* Ploughshares. *Blanco has received
numerous honors for his writings and performances, including an honorary doctorate from Macalester
College and being named a Woodrow Wilson Visiting Fellow. He is currently working on a full-length
memoir and is collaborating with renowned illustrator Dav Pilkey on a children's book.*

Maggie Mitchell

Love, or Ruins

Tanya, Kelly and Jen were as merciless as the glaring cafeteria lights beneath which they picked at their lunches.

They all sat on one side of the long lunchroom table, for two reasons: first, this preserved their solidarity, preventing them from having to configure themselves in a lopsided triangle which would imply an imbalance, an outcast, a third wheel. Second, it gave them all a clear view of the lunch line, which formed on the left side of the cafeteria and inched along the folded-up wooden bleachers that, when necessary, allowed the room to function as an auditorium or a gymnasium. People idly wedged their gum in the gaps in the bleachers as they passed, under the scrutiny of the three senior girls who combated boredom and self-doubt with withering, all-encompassing cruelty.

People idly wedged their gum in the gaps in the bleachers as they passed, under the scrutiny of the three senior girls who combated boredom and self-doubt with withering, all-encompassing cruelty.

Two seats away on the opposite side of the table sat Maddy Stone, attached neither to these three nor the next cluster of seniors, but striving for the illusion of social competence and acceptability by her proximity to both. As usual, Maddy was reading a book under the table, signaling that her solitude was voluntary, not imposed. But her mouth twitched sometimes when one of the three girls spoke, and her eyes occasionally flickered in Jen's direction, carefully expressionless.

Tanya delicately positioned her unfolded napkin over her lunch tray, indicating that her untouched barbecued beef on a bun was offensive not only to her palate but to her sight. Lifting her eyes to the straggling line, she smiled slightly and nudged Kelly and Jen, to her left and her right. "Gloria," she murmured.

They all fixed their mascara-framed gazes on Gloria, who was unfortunately named. Tall and graceless, mousy-haired, and afflicted with an eternally dripping nose, she was perhaps the least visible member of the senior class. Although nearly all of the forty seniors had known each other since kindergarten, almost nothing was known, to anyone, about Gloria. She arrived on the bus, shuffled quietly and alone from class to class, and departed as she had come. Most people had never spoken to her, however casually; nor had they noticed the omission.

"Getting fat," whispered Tanya, and they examined her carefully. Gloria had been scrawny as a little girl, and adolescence had not softened her; sharp bones protruded aggressively from her ill-fitting clothes. Today she wore what looked like a man's flannel shirt. Where you would ordinarily have observed jutting hipbones, had you looked, there was, instead, a soft curve of flesh.

"That's not fat," said Kelly.

Jen's eyes slid sideways to meet those of her friends. "No," she agreed. "That's pregnant." She could tell Maddy was listening, and avoided catching her eye. Oh, spare me, she said to Maddy in her head. She can't hear us.

Maddy, pretending to read, was still preoccupied with the central fact: Gloria Post, of all people, was pregnant. *How?* Gloria Post, of all people, had a secret life.

The three girls began to laugh, discreetly at first and then exploding, collapsing at last in helpless tears. By the end, they hardly knew what they were laughing at.

Head tilted down, eyes on her imitation-leather sneakers, Gloria moved steadily forward, her free-lunch ticket pressed in her damp palm.

Maddy, pretending to read, was still preoccupied with the central fact: Gloria Post, of all people, was pregnant. *How?* Gloria Post, of all people, had a secret life.

The girls' laughter re-erupted the following day, fourth period, during English. Mrs. Mallott considered asking them what was so funny but, out of sheer cowardice, backed down, genuinely afraid of what they might say. Gloria—whose silence had long since relegated her to the so-called "dumb" classes—was in Social Studies, at the time, and did not hear them. The PA system crackled to life: "Will Gloria Post please report to the nurse's office immediately," intoned Mrs. Andrews, the main office secretary. Gloria rose silently, her face flushed with dread, knowing that Mrs. Andrews never said anything just once. The appalling sentence would come again. "Will Gloria Post," Mrs. Andrews repeated more loudly, "please report to the nurse's office at once." She stressed the last words, as if she perceived Gloria's hesitation; scandal was implicit in her tone.

Gloria gathered up her books awkwardly, dropping and ignoring a pencil, and stumbled from the room. Mr. Garner, in whom pity for the girl (he, too, had been an unpopular teenager) battled disgust with her incessant sniffling, waited quietly until she accidentally slammed the door behind her. At this point he raised his eyebrows and resumed his lecture. The remaining students, many of whom had risen before dawn to milk cows, shifted slightly in their seats and continued gazing out the window or doodling marijuana leaves in their notebooks.

In the green-tiled hallway, Gloria considered flight.

If you wanted to walk right out the front door of the school, she thought, there was nothing to stop you. You could go—she paused, mentally sweeping the landscape of the village. You could go back in the woods, where village kids got high before school. You could go down to the river, where—where—(she drew her mind back from the river). Or you could go out to the highway, and hope—against the odds—to catch a ride from someone who didn't know who you were. (A ride to where?) But looking up, she found without surprise that her dutiful feet had led her, not to the front door, but to the nurse's office. She fought back a wave of sickness, and stepped in.

"Ah, Gloria Post," said Mrs. Holleran, the school nurse. "Glooo-ria Post." Mrs. Holleran, often at a loss for words, had developed the habit of turning people's names into impromptu little songs as a substitute for conversation. In this case she would have liked to end it at that: she had no relish for her task. Frankly, she was as reluctant to hear Gloria's story as Gloria, she imagined, would be to tell it. So: "Gloooo-ria, Gloria Post," she sang inanely, glancing at Gloria's file, which until now had contained nothing but immunization records. "Why don't you sit down, hon," she said, and Gloria sank onto the green padded bed along the wall, still clutching her books. "We've—ah—had a report," began Mrs. Holleran, pretending to busy herself at her desk, unwilling to risk meeting Gloria's eyes. "Someone has brought it to our attention that you—ah—that you might be in a tough situation. I'm sure they had only your best interests in mind. It was—it was a parent," she added, perhaps unnecessarily, "It doesn't matter who. But we do need to follow up on—on what they said," she faltered, wishing she had planned her speech.

Gloria kept her eyes on the floor, tracing the brown and cream swirls in the beige tiles.

Just say it, Mrs. Holleran instructed herself. Stop torturing the poor girl. "Gloria, is it true that you're pregnant? I have to ask." Why do I have to ask, she was wondering. Playground injuries, upset stomachs, menstrual cramps, headaches—bandaids and aspirin—those were her territory. But pregnancy? Surely that was not the business of the school nurse.

Gloria said nothing.

"Gloria, my dear girl, you're going to have to answer me. You can't hide from this," said Mrs. Holleran, who for some reason never doubted that the report was true, however unlikely. "You're not making this any easier for yourself." Or for me, she thought, with a twinge of irritation.

Gloria, who was not listening, still said nothing. So far, this was the extent of her plan.

The bus stopped where it always did. Gloria shuffled down a long dirt driveway toward a one-story gray house, all lopsided surfaces and peeling paint. The rusty old washing machine beside the front door had been there so long Gloria didn't even see it.

Set a little farther back from the road was the skeleton of the original farmhouse. A handsome house, with long-shuttered windows and spare, elegant lines, most of it had burned down well before Gloria's birth. The foundation remained, as well as parts of all four walls, the back door, and a treacherously unstable section of the first floor. Gloria's father had been born there; the farm had been different then. For generations the family had been slowly selling off parcels of the land in order to keep the rest afloat, and now little remained. The current house skulked in the shadow of the old.

Doug Post sat at the kitchen table, his big rough hands cupped around a coffee mug, his gaze drawn down into the dark liquid—which was never just coffee anymore, Gloria knew. "Better get them clothes changed and head on out to the barn," he ordered, without turning his eyes to his daughter. On the whole, Gloria did not particularly resemble her mother: but she had the same dark eyes, or at least Doug Post thought so, and he could hardly bear to look at them. Gloria's mother had abandoned the farm, not to mention her family; Gloria, who was a good girl, would not. "Mark's out there on his own today. My back's been real bad. Worth his weight, that boy. Go on, now."

In truth, Doug seldom made it out to the barn, these days. He relied increasingly on his hardworking, efficient hired man, although the neighbors wondered how he afforded this luxury. Gloria helped with the feeding, and sometimes with the milking; she cooked for her father, and made a stab at keeping the house. He did not name to himself her other role, the one that had come to matter most.

Doug didn't see Gloria leave the room, but he felt the air close around her absence. Gloria would save him, he believed. She was tough. You wouldn't guess it, but she was. And she loved him.

Tanya, Jen and Kelly often went into Grandburg after school, because Tanya had a car, and they could. Compared to tiny Bayview, the town acquired a certain glamour: it held out the possibility that you might meet someone you had not seen before, go into a store you'd never noticed, maybe buy something worth having. But the appeal of the rather grim town was purely relative, and in fact there was little to do there. When they tired of driving around the same blocks looking to see if anyone interesting was also driving around, they tended to end up walking aimlessly through stores. Today, they found themselves wandering the aisles of a drug store, deriding the more lurid shades of nail polish, spraying passersby with perfume samplers, and skillfully pocketing candy they would never eat. They mocked products designed for various unthinkable disorders—unguents for hemorrhoids and something called jock itch, wart remover, treatments for foot fungus.

Doug didn't see Gloria leave the room, but he felt the air close around her absence. Gloria would save him, he believed. She was tough.

And then they paused before the diapers. Side by side, all three contemplated the wide-eyed, cartoonish infants gazing at them from dozens of plastic diaper packages. "We should get her some," said Tanya matter-of-factly. Stooping to a low shelf, she picked up the biggest bag she could find.

"Who?" said Kelly, blankly. Her mind had been elsewhere.

"Gloria, of course," said Tanya. "And then let's get some wrapping paper for it," she added, a plan evolving rapidly in her mind.

Tanya's period was late. Earlier she had surreptitiously purchased a home-pregnancy test. Gloria's diapers were, in part, an act of defiance: I dare you, Tanya taunted fate. I dare you to ruin my fucking life.

Clutching the unwieldy bag with sharp, perfectly manicured nails, Tanya headed toward the wrapping paper aisle, smiling her usual mocking smile. Jen and Kelly followed in her wake, guessing nothing.

They wrapped the present in Tanya's garage. The paper featured pastel birds with festoons of curling ribbon draping festively from their beaks; it was designed for baby showers, appropriately. They would have to deliver the package to her house, the girls had decided, since obviously it could not be brought to school. No one had the slightest idea where Gloria lived: out in the country somewhere, was all they knew. The phone book listed several Posts, and so provided no help.

"She takes the bus," Kelly pointed out. "We could find out which bus, and follow it. You know, discreetly." This struck her as a rather tedious proposition, but she was eager to bring the discussion to an end. She was in a hurry to get home, but couldn't say so. Even more pressingly, Kelly wanted to tell her friends about a momentous development in her life: she had lost her virginity, the last of the three to do so. But since she had lost it to Drew Stevens, who happened to be Tanya's boyfriend, she was forced into unnatural secrecy. Drew was a college freshman, and only home on the weekends; this evening, though, he had promised to call her, and she was determined to be there when he did. She was not without guilt: but she loved him, she defended herself fiercely, and Tanya did not. Not really.

"Perfect," said Tanya, impatient for her friends to leave so that she could go upstairs with her purchase and end the maddening suspense. "We'll do it tomorrow."

"Gloria," Mrs. Holleran had told the stubborn girl earlier in the day, "you realize we're going to have to notify your parents." She had forgotten that, as the file could have informed her, Gloria had only a father.

Gloria did not lift her eyes from the floor, but she parted her dry lips slightly and uttered the only word Mrs. Holleran was to hear from her: "When?" she asked, her voice low and expressionless.

Mrs. Holleran paused. Was this up to her? She supposed it was. "Next week," she said kindly. "Early next week. To give you a chance to—you know, bring it up yourself. That would be the best thing, you know. They'd rather hear it from you than me, let me tell you!"

Gloria was unnerved by these references to plural parents. She had only the vaguest memories of her mother, who had vanished when she was a small child. She had run away, was what Gloria's father always said, but Gloria assumed there was more to the story. She waited for Mrs. Holleran to tell her she could go, and then, in silence, she did.

Gloria lived at the end of the bus route: had she lived twenty yards down the road, she would have been in another school district. She was the first one on the bus every morning, and the last one off in the afternoon. She liked riding the bus, usually: nothing was expected of her there. Today she slumped in her seat, face to the window, willing the time between here and home to stretch out forever. The village dwindled to nothing; her gaze swept rushing fields, still darkly muddy from the recent snowmelt; dull red barns, stark silos, grubby cows. Farther out in the country, the road narrowed; the farms became smaller, drearier; half the houses were abandoned, roofs sagging, windows agape. Some only looked abandoned, but looping trails of smoke drifting from crumbling chimneys and tricycles stranded in rutted driveways implied a human presence. Gloria kept having

Gloria kept having to remind herself to blink: something inside her seemed to have frozen. Just keep going, she willed the bus. Just keep going. But the bus stopped where it always did.

to remind herself to blink: something inside her seemed to have frozen.

Just keep going, she willed the bus. Just keep going.

But the bus stopped where it always did.

"How was school?" Jen's mother asked as the girl flung her book bag on the island in the kitchen. Mrs. White aimed for a bright, cheerful tone of voice, expressing genuine interest in her daughter's day, but she had consumed too many gin and tonics to perform this successfully.

"Hell on earth, as usual," said Jen. "Looks like your day wasn't so hot either."

"Your father won't be joining us for dinner this evening, I'm afraid," said Mrs. White, trying not to slur. "But"—she took a deep breath, changing the subject—"I did call the school today, about that unfortunate girl." She smiled.

"God, that was you?" said Jen. "Why do I tell you anything? That was none of your goddamned business."

"Someone had to do it," said Mrs. White primly. "The school has a responsibility to the other students…."

"Right," said Jen, her voice dripping scorn. "Like Gloria Post is really going to corrupt us all."

She stormed upstairs to study her college acceptance letters, for the hundredth time. Jen was planning to go very far away, as far away as she could go. Deb White replenished her drink and contemplated her husband's absence.

"But"—she took a deep breath, changing the subject—"I did call the school today, about that unfortunate girl." She smiled. "God, that was you?" said Jen. "Why do I tell you anything?"

Kelly positioned the pink phone beside her on the bed before spreading out her homework, to which she then half-heartedly applied herself. She had never felt such a dizzying combination of excitement, fear, guilt, desire. In her mind, she called it love. It distracted her hopelessly from her French exercises, and made trigonometry quite impossible.

She planned to answer the phone halfway through the third ring. It never occurred to her that he would not call.

Tanya sat on the bathroom floor, thinking. She had already compared the bands on the little strip to the diagrams in the instructions; she had bundled all the evidence back into the plastic drug store bag, which she intended to smuggle out of the house and dispose of elsewhere. Now there were plans to be made. It made sense to act quickly: the sooner this problem was made to disappear, the sooner it would be possible to pretend it had never happened.

It occurred to her that she despised Drew. Not that she had ever exaggerated or romanticized her feelings for him: he was a catch, and she had caught him. But now she resolved to be rid of him. Soon enough she would graduate, and then the future would begin: she would have no use for Drew. Coldly, she foresaw the trajectory of his life: sooner or later he would flunk out of college; he would come back to town and apply himself half-heartedly to some mid-level position in his father's business, marry some girl as pretty and vacant as he was, and begin to thicken at the middle....

That girl would not be Tanya. What Tanya loved was some future Tanya, a Tanya who did not yet exist—who could not exist, she believed, in Bayview—but whose potential she had always sensed. She wasn't going to give up this easily.

Unbidden, a memory surfaced: the memory Jen had been trying, all day, to suppress. Sophomore year, she remembered, Gloria Post had been in her English class. Mr. Donnelly had required everyone to write a story; the stories, once complete, were deposited in a cardboard box in the front of the room, and for two days the class did nothing but read each other's fictions, randomly selecting manuscripts from the box. Jen waded through athletic triumphs, the deaths of beloved pets and grandmothers, gruesome, badly spelled murder fantasies. What idiots, she thought, resenting for the millionth time the accident of birth that had made her a student at Bayview

Central, K–12, doomed to the same dreary hallways and drearier classmates for thirteen endless years.

And then she drew Gloria's story. She almost put it back, on the assumption that it would be as dull and insubstantial as Gloria herself. But Mr. Donnelly was looking, and so she grimaced and walked back to her desk with the surprisingly thick manuscript.

Gloria's heroine was shy, tall, awkward, friendless. No one understood her. She was lonely, unhappy. And then, one day, a handsome, charming movie star came to town—inexplicably, for the town in the story was indistinguishable from Bayview, which did not tend to be frequented by the rich and famous. The heroine of Gloria's story encountered him by chance, and they struck up a secret friendship—which blossomed, predictably enough, into

What idiots, she thought, resenting for the millionth time the accident of birth that had made her a student at Bayview Central, K–12, doomed to the same dreary hallways and drearier classmates for thirteen endless years.

romance. He saw her "real" self—the self whose existence no one else even suspected. What's more, as he smoothed her mousy hair back from her half-hidden face, he recognized her beauty. Her secret. When he left, he took her with him, and everyone was sorry.

It was Jen's own fantasy, more or less. Here it was rendered baldly, earnestly, poignantly, without a hint of irony. Jen felt her face burning, and lowered her head to let her hair fall forward. She snuck a sideways glance at Gloria, slumped at a desk two rows over. Gloria, as always, was sniffling; she was flipping through someone else's story with apparent boredom. Glancing up, she happened to catch Jen's eye.

A flash of connection shot between them. For a fleeting moment, Jen strove to imagine Gloria's life.

But later, she strove even harder to forget her lapse. Empathy felt dangerous.

Maddy Stone sat at her tiny desk in the back room at Jude's, trying to focus on *Hamlet*. Music from the bar drifted through the thin wall: "There's a tear in my beer," Hank Williams sang for the millionth time, to Maddy's great annoyance.

She was trying not to think about Jude, her mother: an earlier, unfamiliar Jude, but one who must have existed: a pregnant teenager. Disgraced. Disowned? Later, encumbered with a fatherless baby. Together, they had left everyone behind: disappeared. Or so Maddy assumed: Jude refused to tell her the story. It wasn't worth telling, she insisted.

She fixed her eyes on the page before her. Hamlet entreated his father's ghost.

Gloria wore her barn clothes, but she did not go to the barn. Instead, she stepped through the free-standing back door to the ruins of the old house. Since childhood she had known of a spot where the jagged walls provided shelter from the wind and rain, and protected from the view of both house and barn. She tucked herself into this corner, beside the remains of an old fireplace. She pulled her jacket tightly around her and placed her gloved hands on her swollen abdomen. Leaning her head back, she looked up at the ceiling, and the just-budding treetops beyond it. It was funny, she always thought, what burned and what didn't. Entire rooms had vanished without a trace: but here, just at eye level, was a scrap of wallpaper, its cream and gold pattern easily discernible. And above, a chandelier dangled from the lacy ceiling, supporting a perfect bird's nest and a vast network of cobwebs.

Gloria deliberately turned her thoughts to Mark Brady, the hired man, upon whom, her father believed, their lives depended. He was good with the animals, hard-working, dependable. He had the farm running better than it had for years—as efficiently as possible, in the circumstances. He had dark hair, a straight nose, blue eyes, clear-cut cheekbones. He looked, in fact, remarkably like the movie star in her long ago story. But he almost never spoke. He was rumored to be—well, not quite all there, Gloria thought, avoiding the cruel words she had sometimes overheard. But she doubted this: there was something in his eyes that suggested otherwise.

And he did, on occasion, speak. Rain coming, he would say, with a knowing glance at sky; or, must be lunchtime. These cryptic statements, Gloria supposed, proved nothing.

But: I love you, he had also said, maybe the fifth time he had led her to his trailer on the other side of the fields. And then, ambiguously: Doug wants me to stay.

He had his own reasons, Gloria thought, for not speaking, and for letting people think what they thought. She suspected him of having a secret past. His skills qualified him for a better job than this one, and his looks for a more desirable girl than Gloria Post. He was not from around here; where he had come from was one of the things he did not say. At first this mystery had seemed romantic; later she had wondered if it would make more sense to see it as sinister.

Was it possible, Gloria wondered, that he loved her? At first she had hoped so: and love, even from such an uncertain source, had seemed something worth having. Mark's silence freed her to invent him. But his eyes, which she studied for clues, raised doubts: not so much for what they revealed, but what they seemed to hide. She wasn't sure that love could be at once so mute and so circumspect. But Gloria was in unfamiliar territory: no one had ever spoken these words to her, and they were not unlike a foreign language. In themselves the syllables conveyed nothing very clear, but it seemed possible that, by listening carefully to inflection, to timbre, she might unearth the truth.

One thing, she thought, as a squirrel wandered into her sanctum and paused to examine her, was all too clear. If she disappointed Mark (this was how she phrased it), he would leave. If he left, the farm would collapse, and her father with it. She would have completed the destruction set in motion by her mother, years ago.

Unless, as she had begun to wonder—questioning the story on which Doug, bitterly, had raised her—it was her mother who had been betrayed.

Where had her mother gone? If her father knew, he had never hinted. Where could you go?

Increasingly, it seemed to Gloria that the solution to her own predicament was bogged down in unanswerable questions: why had her mother— Cheryl, her name was—why had Cheryl deserted her husband, her little girl? Had she loved them? For what had she traded them?

What lay behind Mark's unspeaking face? What secrets, what love, or what nameless thing that called itself love but was not?

And the new inchoate presence, the one inside her: what claim did this being have on all of them? What unbreathed entreaty did her swelling flesh embody?

An echo of the laughter of the awful girls in the cafeteria drifted into her mind, and she hastily shut it down. There would be no going back to school, that much was clear. But what, then. She had come here to think. There had to be a way. Already she would have been missed: even this brief lapse had the power to set in motion something irrevocable.

Tanya, sleepless that night, impulsively rejected the diaper plan even before she knew that Gloria would not be on the bus, tomorrow or ever. For months the package rode around in the trunk of her car, increasingly battered. Not until after graduation did she at last toss it by night into a dumpster behind the school, with a relief that seemed disproportionate to the action. The gaudily wrapped parcel had acquired associations over the months: treacherous Kelly, hated Drew, the abortion—all were caught up in the festive pastels. But what also remained was an image of Gloria, sniffling and secretive. In vanishing, Gloria had become visible. Tanya was not the only one she haunted.

Gloria looked up at the ghostly old chandelier. Defiant, it clung through generations to the charred rafters, refusing the fate ordained by fire.

Surely, she thought wildly, not everything has to burn.

Maggie Mitchell's first novel, Pretty Is, *will be published by Henry Holt in 2015. Her short fiction has appeared in a number of literary magazines, including* New Ohio Review, American Literary Review, *and* Green Mountains Review. *Her story "It Would Be Different If" has been anthologized in* The Bedford Introduction to Literature. *She teaches English and creative writing at the University of West Georgia.*

Cheney Crow

The Ear of Her Dog

In the photo on my desk
the child's holding the ear of a dog.

She cracked almonds between two stones
carefully, like she poured water in tiny cups.

Almond trees, cherries, vineyards
The world she knew.

Around me now, noise of typing,
Screaming phones.

To touch one triggers memory in my body
of her father's voice,

I am holding a gun to my head.

After those words,
the sound of a single shot.

Then silence
louder than the world.

And she came walking,
holding the ear of her dog.

A Doctor Reminds Me of London

Was there a blow to this eye?

The doctor asked. Of course
I thought of you
and the house on Kenway Road,
just up from the pub.

Did you say yes?

Everyone knew there was no
accident. Bandaged
six weeks, the eye
showed escalation from private bruises,
knocks to the public curb.

The damage is irreversible.

One night a bobby knocked at our
door. He asked for a cleaning rag,
told a red-faced man beside him
to apologize to me. The man mumbled
he had urinated on our gate, then knelt
to clean it under the bobby's watchful eye.
An eye that saw my bandage, but not you.

Cheney Crow believes in art as expression and engagement. She has worked as a sculptor and musician in France and Spain, in various jobs in England, as a linguist at the University of Texas, photographer and translator. Her favorite degrees are her Sarah Lawrence College BA and recent Warren Wilson MFA. Her poems have recently appeared in The Cortland Review *and* HEArt (Human Equity Through Art).

Jennifer Balachandran

Cold Sore

time again for my annual
face herpes   the time my mouth becomes
an expressionist painting   shows
my latent ugly on the outside
so I can finally say   sometimes
I hate my kids
for the way they need
life as much as I ever did
though to me it seems like more
and how I notice a snotty nose
before light shining through leaves

Then there was the one who said

Then there was the one who said
you're the queen bee, repeatedly,
so I slept with him because I was drunk and also
for some reason it turned me on, though of course later, upon
further reflection, it dawned on me
the queen is the bee I'd least
like to be, gorged on the royal jelly,
pumping out babies not ever
getting to leave the hive. What kind
of a life is that? But then
it dawned on me that some part of my brain
must be tiny as hers, subject
to that kingly imperative.

Before Worship

I retrieved the loaves from the downstairs freezer
and laid them in the sacristy, end to end,
leaving plenty of time to thaw.
Solid cold domes of crust.
They needed to be soft
for everyone to take and eat.
It was my job. They paid me.
I never attended worship,
but I set out the bread
and I liked doing that—
which was the extent of it.

it just doesn't seem right

it just doesn't seem right
to be coughing pubes when you pick your child up
from school   that sweet release
of an irresponsible hour becoming
a chain that whips you   the air humid
the clouds too puffy to move
then the bell rings and the building
ejaculates children   if someone whispers freedom
in your ear   it only turns you on
because it isn't real

Jennifer Balachandran has had work published in Flycatcher, *and is a contributor to the interactive social media poetry project* Electronic Corpse: Poems from a Digital Salon. *She also posts her own poems regularly on her blog at flindermouse.com.*

Jericho Brown

ESL

You come with a little
Black string tied
Around your tongue
Knotted to remind
Where you came from
And why you left
Behind photographs
Of people whose
Names need no
Pronouncing. How
Do you say God
Now that the night
Rises sooner? How
Dare you wake to work
Before any alarm?
I am the man asking,
The great grandson
Made so by the dead
Tenant farmers promised
A plot of land to hew.
They thought they could
Own the dirt they were
Bound to. In that part
Of the country, a knot
Means something you
Get after getting knocked
Down, and story means
Lie. In your part
Of the country, class

Means school, this room
Where we practice
Words like *rope*, because
We hope to undo your
Tongue, so you can tell
A story or make
A promise or grow a lie.

Atlantis

What I stole I took with ease
Though the sun is the eye
Of regret that burns on women

Who bend for wages they make.
What I lost holding my breath
While those women wallowed

In the name of Jesus underwater,
I watched from this new land
Of waxed legs, where God's good

Eye beams, all our teeth white, all
Our canyons right, sand and sea
Shimmering like some evening

Gown of a wealthy woman with
No noticed want, no reason
To believe the work a grudge

And good distance can do once
You leave a dangerous city
Of women below sea level alone.

What I remember about New Orleans
I never touched—the women,
Even the youngest call you baby.

Big, Fine

Long ago, we used two words for the worth of a house, a car,
A woman—all the same to men who claimed them: things
To be entered, each to experience wear and tear with time.

And greater than the love for these was the strange little grin
One man offered another saying, *You lucky. You got you a big,*
Fine _____. Hard to imagine—so many men waiting

On each other to be recognized, every right tooth in our
Naming mouths ready like the syllables of a very short
Sentence, so many of us crying *mine*, like infants who grab

For what must be beautiful since someone else saw it.

Jericho Brown is the recipient of fellowships from the Radcliffe Institute for Advanced Study at Harvard University and the National Endowment for the Arts. His poems have appeared or are forthcoming in The Nation, The New Yorker, The New Republic, *and* The Best American Poetry. *His first book,* Please, *won the American Book Award, and his second book,* The New Testament, *was published by Copper Canyon Press. He is an assistant professor in the creative writing program at Emory University.*

Alan Shapiro

In A Bad Time

When we first met
and for a good time
after there was this
voice you'd speak
my name with that
became the name
I didn't know
was mine until
I heard you speak it,
the name that when
not spoken by you
as it seldom is now
is—whoever else
might speak it—not
a name at all and,
while it isn't, never was
except inside
the breathless echo
chamber of remembering
how you sounded
speaking it with
such unstinted
and abundant wanting
that there is no
end now to its
diminishment, the echo
of it grown so
barely audible
that the faintness of it is

itself an inverse
echo of the very
fullness of the times
you hadn't said it
to me yet, but would,
and did, for so long
and so richly—how
could I not confuse
the eager pitch and timbre
of it on your lips
for what I was?
Or not know
what name it is
you speak now
when you're speaking it?

The Pig

The 1950's of her dream persisted
Into the 1960's,
Confident at first,

Despite the first awakenings around it,
Even a little smug,
Unthreatened, but then as more and more awoke

It grew confused, mystified, furious,
Retreating to a last redoubt—
Part farce,

Part suicide mission—
Of her wanting us
Never to help her with what she did alone

While wanting every one of us
To see her do it every evening
As her fork scraped uneaten scraps

Down the hole of the disposal
That she called the pig
And flipped the switch

To hear it churn
All she'd done for us
To nothing,

The dishes scoured and sparkling on the rack,
The tabled scrubbed to chilly radiance,
The floor swept,

She never wanting us, not once, not
Ever, to help her do it,
Not even on the nights she herself refused to do it,

Had had enough
Already and would sit there
At the bomb site of the table

Cigarette burning down between her fingers,
Untouched cup of coffee steaming
Till it didn't,

She wanting us to see her stare at nothing, see
Her not care if we saw
How she had gone away

Like food scraps down the pig
Of nowhere we could follow
Where the dream churned

On itself down through the void
Of its persistence
Among the wreckage all the waking up had wrought.

Interrogation

Impresario of all, O holy this
who art that
        who
disposes me to think
whatever happened up to this very instant
had to have happened
for this couple in angelic bright
white headbands, white sweat suits and sneakers
to be jogging down the street
I just now happen to be turning up on—
O Tummler of tummlers, you who fill me with wonder
for the uncountable,
unaccountably entangled
chains of how
behind the chance
encounter: the big Ta-Da! of which
is what, the damaged bodies—
the too large head for the little torso of the man,
and how the woman's whited over
blind eyes fix on nothing
as she lumbers in a herky
jerky downhill faltering
that makes her, leaning forward,
wobble side to side
as in a cross wind
on a tight rope
over a darkness they both seem on the verge
of tumbling into
for the universe's entertainment as they stumble by.

Or is it, as they stumble by,
how their fingers, cupped
together, touch
so loosely that
it's more a readiness to touch
than touch, and thus impossible to tell
just who is guiding whom,

so I should what, be happy for them now,
so I can think it's somehow all okay
because you have this once, almighty ham,
merciless cut up,
permitted me
by accident a glimpse
in damage of a little tenderness
to make more merciful your mercy, or your cruelty crueler
as hand in hand they vanish round the corner?

Mother Charon

What goes by is being shaped by what has gone by
in the continuous disappearing act of being here so still
inside the speeding car behind the rolled up window while

the cataclysmic feeling of a doomsday clock ticks through the bland
voices reasoning about the same news she punches button
after button to escape from to the shelter of a song

that isn't there   only shadows flickering down through trees
we're passing under   up and down my arm like something I can almost feel
until I try to feel it and it flickers across the hand I try to feel it with

the trolley on the right ahead of us appears to stop beside us
without stopping running side by side a moment going nowhere
full of people looking out at me as if I am not looking in at them

until the trolley's sinking as we go uphill   up above the hats and staring
glasses and now even the sparking wires before it all starts to rise again
as we descend and the going faster pushes me back hard against the seat

What goes by keeps going by   the clock ticks probabilities
of what they'd never do to us because of what
we'd never do to them   because she's sick of it all

sick and tired do I hear her do I   of running and doing
for me for everyone for no appreciation   nothing
pink lipstick rifled from her purse now in her free hand

slashing air   a cigarette between two fingers of the other
on the wheel releasing faint spirals of smoke that hang
suspended there so still between her face and the windshield

the world is rushing at and sliding over while the radio
sings at last   come fly with me come fly come fly away
and the trolley is again beside us with different faces now

not seeing me see them appearing not to move because
we're moving at the same speed through the same moment
of whatever's coming toward us to be gone.

Alan Shapiro's new book, Reel to Reel, *was published in April by University of Chicago Press. His last book,* Night of the Republic, *was a finalist for both the National Book Award and the Griffin Prize.*

Magician. Ink & watercolor on paper, 10"x 7". Lawrence Yang.

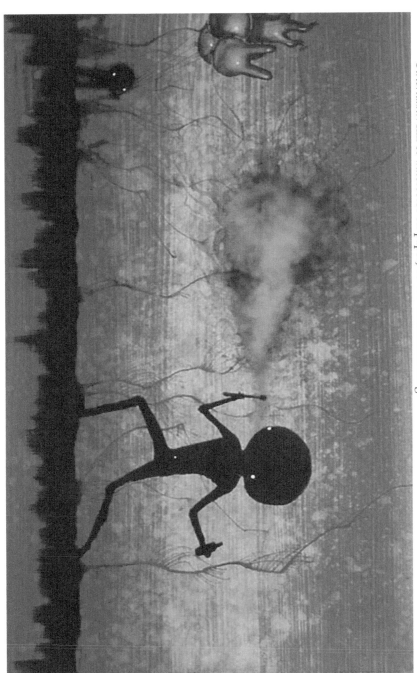

Firebreather. Ink & watercolor on paper, 10" x 7". Lawrence Yang.

Date. Ink, watercolor, & gouache on paper, 15"x 11". Lawrence Yang.

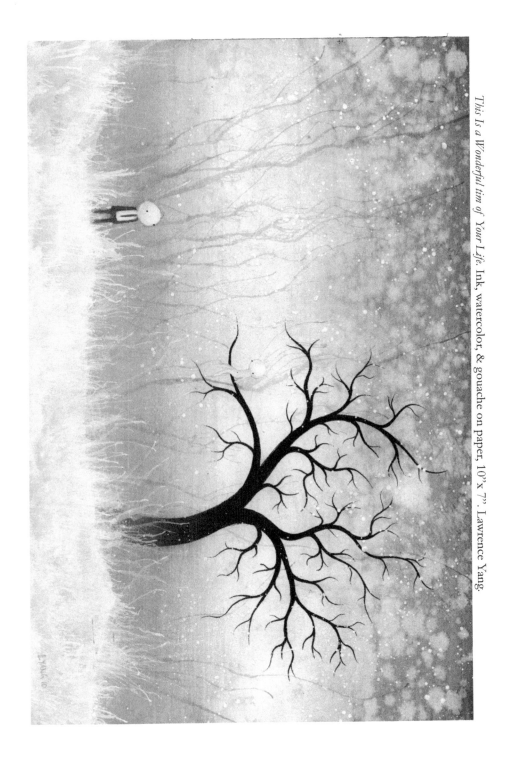

This Is a Wonderful tim of Your Life, Ink, watercolor, & gouache on paper, 10"x 7". Lawrence Yang.

Curious Giraffe, Ink, watercolor, & gouache on paper, 5"x 5". Lawrence Yang.

Pig Explorer. Ink, watercolor, & gouache on paper, 5"x 5". Lawrence Yang.

Mecha Shaun. Ink, watercolor, & gouache on paper, 12"x 9". Lawrence Yang.

Pig. Ink, watercolor, & gouache on paper, 10"x 7". Lawrence Yang.

Denise Duhamel

Post-Apocalyptic

My grandfather tells me about the days of Xbox, how the underground bunkers and vaults on his screen predicted technology's demise as he played. He and the other kids didn't get it—how could they have? My grandfather was only ten when the electricity stopped working, when the cold food in the supermarkets spoiled because the men with guns wouldn't let the looters get to it in the dark.

It's hard for me to imagine my orphaned grandfather learning "real" war and fighting with the others until all the bullets on earth were gone. He still holds on to his antique gun, his antique views about people. It's hard for me to imagine a time when people were so caught up on identity, who was called a man and who was called a woman and who made love to whom. It's hard for me to imagine a time when there was something called snow or a temperature so cold that people wore coats. But I've seen the pictures. It's hard for me to imagine an ocean moving with waves where the greenhouse is now.

That's why I started this diary. Someday my grandchildren might want to know what it was like for me. Our village is known for its sheep—the meat, the wool that we use as filler for pillows. We don't like fighting, but we do have bows and arrows in case of wild animals that sometimes come from the highway, a ribbon of concrete that is decorated by murals. Some say the animals spring from the paintings of animals, but I don't believe it.

On a typical day, we get up at dawn and feed ourselves, then the sheep. We eat oats and vegetables when we can get them. We hike to the well to carry water in buckets. We take care of the sick with special plants. My parents have forbidden me to write down the plants' names or where they grow, as people from other villages might rob us. I think my parents are a bit paranoid, but I respect them and besides, they might read this. There are tribes that play music; tribes that gamble with pebbles; tribes that just like to run as fast as they can. There are the rich people, the ones with horses. They like to show off. We drift off to sleep when it gets dark. In the middle of the night, some of us wake and gather to tell our dreams. Then we sleep again.

Once in a while we'll meet a nomadic wanderer who can tell a good story. About a forgotten warehouse full of rolls of old paper towels. About a castle with metal stairs and benches and mysterious plants made of plastic. These plants will never die and some, like me, consider them magic. In the castle are many rooms, the front walls of which are made with clear glass. These castles, my uncle explains, used to be something called malls. I want to be a wanderer when I get older so I can visit the castles.

War

Pink:
Do you even remember why we're here?

Blue:
To win the war.

Pink:
But what do we win?

Blue:
I forgot.

And so it went, troops on both sides of The Binary War growing tired and confused. Even the Androgynous were sick of vigils and sit-ins. Pink and Blue Soldiers defected, trading uniforms. Some burned their britches, opting to wear only white like eighteenth century children of all genders who wore dresses until they were six, the time of their first haircuts. Others MIA wore only black or khaki.

The sergeants on both sides ignored the past. During World War I, the rule was pink, a decided and strong color, for the boys; and blue, delicate and dainty, for the girls. Pink was closer to red, the bloodline. Blue closer to the Virgin Mary. Even during the Depression, Filene's, Halle's and Marshall Field all sold pink to masculine toddlers and blue to feminine ones. It wasn't until 1940 when the colors switched and no historian can definitively say why. Jo Paoletti of the University of Maryland, a longtime specialist on the topic, says, "It could have easily gone the other way."

Femslash

Laverne had always been a "tomboy," or so her parents said. Skinned knees, fistfights, saving her paper route money to buy the girly girls frou frou. The "L" embroidered on all her sweaters stands for more than Laverne. She wears boxers under her poodle skirt as she waits out the conservative 1950s.

Shirley is the kind of girl Laverne has been waiting for all her life—a goody-two-shoes with a perky smile. Plus she lives in the same apartment!

One Friday night after a few beers, Shirley and Laverne lie on Shirley's bed, overworked, too tired to get ready for their bowling date. They talk about everything under the sun until they get to sex. Shirley insists that she would "never, well, you know…" then stammers and turns red.

"I don't vo-dee-o-doe-doe," Shirley finally says.

Laverne replies, "Oh, I think you *do* vo-dee-o."

Shirley grabs her stuffed "Boo Boo Kitty" and hides her face. Laverne pops open two more bottles of Shotz.

When Lenny and Squiggy knock on the door, Laverne and Shirley cover each other's mouths trying not to laugh.

"Shh…" Shirley whispers. "Don't answer."

Shirley has an epiphany. She has never vo-dee-o-doe-dooed because she never wanted to vo-dee-o with a man.

The two women look into each other's eyes until they hear Lenny say, "Come on. Maybe the girls are already at the Pizza Bowl."

Then, together Shirley and Laverne do it their way and make all their dreams come true.

Denise Duhamel's most recent book of poetry Blowout *(University of Pittsburgh Press, 2013) was a finalist for the National Book Critics Circle Award and winner of a 2014 Paterson Poetry Prize. Her other books include* Ka-Ching! *(Pittsburgh, 2009),* Two and Two *(Pittsburgh, 2005), and* Queen for a Day: Selected and New Poems *(Pittsburgh, 2001). The guest editor for* The Best American Poetry 2013, *she is a professor at Florida International University in Miami.*

Stuart Dischell

Excerpt from Walking the Walls of Paris

1
From the Heart of Paris

All over Paris white feathers of seed fluff drift down, and in some quarters pigeons are molting. Pale cones of brown flowers and rarer purple ones blossom from the chestnut trees. On the first of May, children sell them on the boulevards to raise funds for schools and charities—a vestige of the pagan in their young and ritualistic hands. In the warm afternoon, the streets are crowded with casually and elegantly dressed people. I am glad to be among them, following my desire, walking along the paths of the vanished walls of the city.

Over the course of my life, I have changed from someone who knows hardly a soul in Paris to a person living in expanding circles. I can never stay long enough, but because I visit frequently, I fall happily and immediately into my routine of writing most mornings until I can no longer sit still. Then I go out walking the streets along or near where the old fortifications stood, remarking to myself when I am inside, outside, or between them—*intra, extra,* and *inter muros.* Exhilarated but fatigued, I usually dine alone, sleep for an hour or two, and then go out again. Sometimes I enjoy a *nuit blanche,* a white night, when I go to bed at dawn.

In a time of personal chaos—the break-up of my marriage, my father's decline and death, and having my heart broken in subsequent relationships—the paths of the walls give me direction, keep me on my feet.

Paris and what were once its city walls are my constant subject. As if following the trail of missing persons, I look for evidence of what is no longer there. In a time of personal chaos—the break-up of my marriage, my father's decline and death, and having my heart broken in subsequent relationships—the paths of the walls give me direction, keep me on my feet. Or do they take me in circles? Although there is much experience to be gained just by walking in random fashion, to find Paris by getting lost in it, for me the pleasure of exploration is the unearthing of the past within the present, to understand where it is I stand. As I follow the traces and uncover the vestiges of the walls, I see Paris in its many layers like a map with fold-back transparencies that depict the city over the course of the ages.

On these streets, I am a hopeless case. I sense immanence on every corner, and in every part of the city a block or two quickly leads me somewhere different. I feel purposeful even in my daydreams, joyful even when I am cranky. Of course there are bad days in Paris, too. The Francophobes and scoffers enjoy hearing of them, but for me Paris is the kind of companion that, after faulting, I immediately find remarkable again, and in those moments of doubt, the play of light on the sidewalk or an acknowledging nod from a tradesman reminds me why I keep returning to walk this city.

It has become a joke to my friends back in America that the phrase "in Paris" can be attached like a suffix to any statement I utter.

"The mail is efficient in Paris."

"The bread is good in Paris."

And of course, "There is always somewhere to walk in Paris."

The paths of the five major city walls have traced a map in my brain. They radiate in an off-center, jagged, ovoid bull's eye target that expands from the earliest island settlement to the last incorporation of the modern city. Infrequently tested for defense and on major occasions breached, these fortifications—also known as *Les Enceintes*, the belts—nevertheless impacted the design of Paris' development more than any other events in the history of the city. The streets I walk owe their character to the constructions and subsequent demolitions of these barriers, ramparts, trenches, moats, and gates. Even the word "boulevard" itself derives from the bulwark, the pathway atop the walls.

Built late in the third century, the first wall enclosed the original island village and marked the retreat of the Gallo Romans when unusually cold winters permitted the barbarians to cross frozen rivers and head west. Evidence of other ramparts exists, but it was not until 1200, relatively late by medieval urban standards, that King Philippe Auguste raised the next major walls to protect the city from English attack and ensure Paris and his loot would still be there when he returned from the Third Crusade. The walls could also be used to seal the city, effectively locking people in and keeping bandits and wolves out at night. To accommodate a growing population, Charles V, in the latter half of the fourteenth century, enhanced and expanded the fortifications. He was a man, it is said, who put his faith in walls.

Further extensions by subsequent regents included prosperous new districts on the Right Bank. In 1670, Louis XIV tore down all the walls, and Paris remained an open city until 1785 when the next construction, the most hated of all and among the causes of the Revolution, the Wall of the Farmers General, was erected. A Toll Wall completed during the regency of Louis XVI, its classically designed gates served as collection points for tariffs and taxes, rather than function for the protection of Parisians.

In 1670, Louis XIV tore down all the walls, and Paris remained an open city until 1785 when the next construction, the most hated of all and among the causes of the Revolution, the Wall of the Farmers General, was erected.

Approximately, twenty-two miles in circumference, the final and largest fortification was constructed in the 1840s along what is still the boundary of Paris. Not a wall as much as a pattern of earthen and stone ramparts, *les Fortifs*, as they were affectionately called, are otherwise known as the Wall of 1840 or the Wall of Thiers, named after the redoubtable French politician, Adolphe Thiers, who championed the construction. In the cleared zone beyond where *les Fortifs* had been, the *Peripherique*, the beltway, now befits the present city, surrounding it with a wall of traffic.

Through the maze of central Paris, along downtrodden and still grand boulevards, and at the peripheries of the city, vestiges of these walls remain in alleys and impasses, gardens and courtyards, cellars and parking garages,

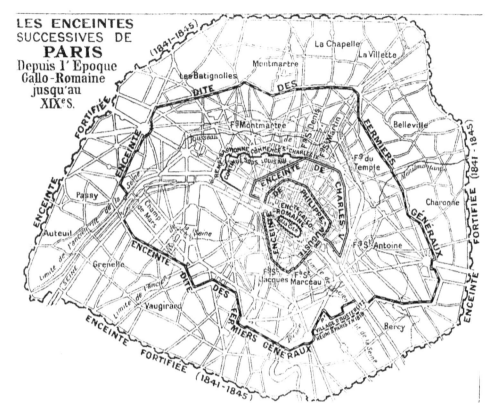

and in the topography of the landscape. In near and distant quarters, I find these towers and arches, columns and gatehouses, bastions and embankments. I enter shops and markets, bars and cafés, betting parlors and brothels, new apartment blocks and one of the reputed oldest houses of Paris where upscale libertines exchange their spouses. I term this "ambient research" and return to Paris as often as I can get away with it.

2
The Genetic Component

My lifelong attraction to Paris and by extension its ancient city walls has a genetic component in the form of my grandparents who arrived at the Gare de l'Est on November 14 of 1910 on a journey by train that took them from Warsaw to Berlin then to Paris. The previous summer in Warsaw, my grandfather Maier encountered my grandmother walking home from work one evening and was so awed by her presence, he followed her back to where she lived. When he knocked at the door, he was dismayed when Berthe, my grandmother's roommate, told him she alone resided there. He waited outside the building until my grandmother emerged the next morning. When she refused to date him, he slept outside her door. Days or weeks went by. The neighbors took notice. After awhile, she got used to having him around. Eventually, she agreed to marriage on the condition that he would take her to live in Paris.

The family story further alleges that along with their hand-baggage, they began their transport with a scuffed trunk taken from the attic of Maier's Aunt Honorata, who had been an actress in the Great Theater of Warsaw. Inside it were blankets and tablecloths, silverware and dishes, pots and pans, nothing of financial value but the stuff that makes a life. Depositing this trunk at the baggage counter of the Berlin Bahnhof had caused them some anxiety. What if it were plundered or sent on the wrong train the next morning or left to sit forever in another station's baggage room? One of these things must have happened because their chest indeed went missing. They were poor and now they were infinitely much poorer at the time they would need simple goods most. My grandfather was a man of lovely ways but bad luck.

He waited outside the building until my grandmother emerged the next morning. When she refused to date him, he slept outside her door.

By the time they concluded making their first agitated then resigned inquiries of the conductors, the baggage handlers, and the baggage room manager, and exited the Gare de l'Est, there were but few horse cabs by the station. Notably, the young couple did not argue.

One is said to have said, "We have only each other now," because in the family stories my uncles or mother would always say, "They had only each other then."

They walked a little ways down the Boulevard Sebastopol. The sympathetic look of a horse reminded her of Kastusheks, the better half of her uncle's plow in Kovno where she lived as a child. Indeed the look of the cab driver reminded her of a Kovnocapbernian as well, which is what in fact he was. The driver asked them in Yiddish if they were going to the Pletzel, "the little place," as the formerly grand Marais district was known to the Central European Jews. He delivered them to his sister's lodging house on the rue des Ecoffes, near or perhaps even inside the same building where my friend Werner now resides.

A few days later my grandparents rented a room around the corner on the rue des Rosiers. At first they slept in their clothing, the lamented trunk having contained their wool blankets. By January, even with the purchase of proper bedclothes, they would be so cold they slept in layers of garments. My grandfather had gotten work sewing as his mother had taught him, in a workshop in the Sentier neighborhood not far away. Having grown up in Warsaw, a capital city, he spoke French well enough to converse at length, and I am told he was a big talker, a family trait no doubt. Before my uncles were born in rapid succession in

Record and bookstore at 34, rue des Rosiers

1914 and 1915, my grandmother Esther worked as a clerk in a dry goods shop on the rue Pavee. Selling mostly to Yiddish speakers, she did not learn much French and what she knew she said in a heavy accent. She pronounced Hotel de Ville as "Utel da Vil."

In the lovely, somewhat deluded state of mind in which one can believe one is a Parisian without really being French, my grandparents considered themselves so. In their manner, she and my grandfather were also Modernists. My grandfather was an artist who had taken up the slightly more practical goal of designing women's clothes. His drawings had a sense of style and color and line about them as if he were well aware of the work of his contemporaries. Was it a spirit of the age or was he that quick a study?

According to my grandmother, Paris was not merely the capital of France or Europe but the only truly civilized place on Earth. Everything was wonderful to them. From the taste of the bread to the wind on the bridges. In gray coats and dark shoes, under a gray sky, above the leaden water, beside the rows of gray buildings and monuments, they were happy to have left the East. They put their hands inside each other's coat pockets and kissed when they thought no one was looking. Although they were my grandparents, they were young and shy. Their five years in Paris would form the habits of thought for their children, grandchildren, and now great grandchildren.

I picture a Saturday evening for them in the summer of 1912. Although the trees are still very green, I see the city in the black and white light of the photographs of the time. The Sabbath is over and the streets of the Marais are teeming with people. Among them, my grandmother and grandfather have stepped out for a walk. She is wearing a dress he has designed and made for her, and I believe it is the one she later wore in her passport photo, the same pointed collar. She is pregnant with my uncle Reney, but she is not yet showing. She is of medium height and has a noble carriage. She is blond and blue eyed and her eye lashes are pale. One might have seen her poverty only in her worn and poorly made shoes. My grandfather had managed to get some luster out of them by rubbing them with coal dust and oil. My grandfather is wearing his only suit, but he has enlivened himself with a tie he had recently bought at Samaritain's department store after being paid the day before. He has a knack of always being attracted to the finest fabric. He is wearing his hat, although he has heard that in America, men are changing the custom. He is smoking a cigarette, another habit he acquired while hanging around the theater in Warsaw.

From their apartment on the rue des Rosiers they walked west and turned the corner on the rue des Hospitalieres St-Gervais and the school where the restaurant Chez Marianne stands today. These are the days before the Great War when the world seemed cohesive and the old empires truculent but content. Like most people on the street, they had no awareness of the wall they strolled beside, whose length ran between the rue des Rosiers and the rue des Francs Bourgeois, and whose towers and stones lurked all around them. And if they did, I do not think they would have made much of it except another example of urban decrepitude.

I imagine what my grandparents' lives would have been like had the horse-cab driver delivered them across the city to Montparnasse where international artists such as Zadkine, Modigliani, Chagall, and Soutine had established themselves. Maier might have hung out with Jules Pascin, who spent his time in the Vavin cafés, often secretly drawing people with a pencil stub and paper hidden in his coat pocket. He might have palled around with Picasso and Apollinaire and like them he might have been accused of stealing the Mona Lisa. He might have stayed in Paris and made love to Kiki while Man Ray was making movies with my favorite poet, Robert Desnos. From what I know, Maier was a practical joker, too, and would have enjoyed the company of the Dadaists and Surrealists. But like many talented

A family on the Paris Express

young people, he did not have the money, luck, or connections to make his way as an artist. He was a handsome impractical man who squandered the little money he earned buying lovely trifles for himself and sometimes his wife and children. He was an avid but luckless gambler because he believed so much he would win, one of the beautiful foolish men of my family. Our hero.

It was while walking in the rue des Rosiers, trying to get some sense of my grandparents' life in Paris that I happened upon the Wall of Philippe Auguste. Construction work was in progress at the apartment building across the street from Goldenberg's restaurant. Through the open *porte* I stopped and peered at the workmen and the last remnants of the building they had cleared. In the back of the debris-strewn lot at the far corner, the demolition had spared a remarkable high heap of old stones, what I would later discover was a section of the Wall of Philippe August the workmen uncovered at the back boundary of the property.

I had held the vaguest notion that Paris must once have been a fortified city. I had seen the chunk that abuts the rue Clovis on the Left Bank and the walls and towers along the rue Jardins-St Paul. I noticed plaques here and there around the city—yet the bull's eye of the pattern had not yet transposed itself for me upon the city map. I was curious what I might find if I followed where the Walls of Paris would take me in the city in this first decade of the new century.

3
First Encounter

Memory tells me, I first encountered the Walls of Paris in 1974 with Denise, my college girlfriend and co-conspirator of my twenties. She had gone to Europe to learn German before matriculating at Tubingen University in the fall. I followed her to alter her plan. At the end of the summer, I flew to Frankfurt, stayed a few days in Marburg where she attended language school, then we hitchhiked on the Autobahn to Hanover where we visited her older sister and Norbert, her sister's German boyfriend. They wouldn't let us sleep together—though I suppose Norbert could care less. I was as eager as he to move us along, and the small apartment had gotten tighter with the arrival of two of his friends who dressed like clowns in wide striped pants and drank hashish they stirred until it melted in their coffee. Norbert smoked his with tobacco. He called it "my piece."

I was six foot one, weighed one hundred and twenty-eight pounds, had crazy hair to my shoulders, a concave chest, and a wildly positive self-image.

Soon it was off to Amsterdam, London, and then, finally, to Paris. I don't remember how we managed to get around and figure out the timetables and ultimately arrive where we went. I had a plan like my grandparents that we would come to Paris by train, but I made the predictable mistake of Americans in Britain like asking for pants instead of trousers. In this case, when the travel agent suggested we go by coach, I thought he meant we would be riding in the coach of a train not a motor coach—another early event in my pattern of misunderstanding.

I brought Denise birth control pills from the U.S. She requested I get them from one of her friends who had the same prescription. I brought a carton of unfiltered Camel cigarettes I was told Europeans preferred to their own dry smokes. I brought in my suitcase the largest jar of peanut

LA PORTE S.ᵀ DENIS.

butter I could find that we used as a bribe to get a fellow student to take our additional suitcases with him from Marburg to Tubingen. I also brought my French-English dictionary and traveler's checks secured with money from selling a guitar that I couldn't play well. I was six-foot-one, weighed one hundred and twenty-eight pounds, had crazy hair to my shoulders, a concave chest, and a wildly positive self-image.

Our first evening in Paris we had eaten supper just beyond the Walls of Charles V, though I did not know it then, in the rue Faubourg St-Denis at Restaurant Julien at that time still a *bouillon*, a humble establishment. After taking our order, the waiter returned with the intention of informing me that the dish I wanted had been sold out, but I could not comprehend what he so rapidly said to me. In mild exasperation, he looked at the Frenchman who shared our part of the table. A working man in a blue smock, the man proclaimed almost as if he were standing up, "Sir, your duck is no more."

I thought he said "dog" and looked perplexed but we thanked him all the same, as did the waiter, and I then ordered *rognons du veau*, what I thought was roast veal rounds, and received a transplant of rare veal kidneys instead. At first, I could not tell the artfully sliced stuff from the mushrooms until I tasted the unmistakable flavor of organ meats. The man confided that his grandfather enjoyed this same dish except the old man prepared his *cuit a morte*, cooked to death. Luckily, my plate had a strong sauce, and with bread I ate it all. Whatever the table wine was, it was good, and we were seated with an adult Frenchman who actually liked and respected us for being college students. We engaged in elementary conversation in both English and French. We shared the wine and nodded our heads. After six years of hard hats and Richard Nixon, we reveled in his company.

A generation after its occupation, Paris was still recovering from the War. In its housing stock and the manner of dress, particularly of working people, reminders of the older way of life were still apparent.

After dinner, Denise and I walked back toward the Grands Boulevards to find the Metro. Ahead of us the Porte St-Denis looked white and spooky in the night. Where had it come from? What did it mean? Surely it was a good omen as I conflated her name with Denis.

In 1974, American travelers thought Paris a charming but dirty city. Despite its famous hotels, many of its lodgings and apartments lacked one or more utilities. The facades of today's sparkling buildings had not yet been scrubbed of centuries of soot. The Forum of Les Halles project had recently cleared one of the city's oldest, best loved, and most infested quarters. On the Left Bank, the once dense residential neighborhoods around the Place d'Italie already had been razed. The Platte de Beaubourg had been a parking lot for decades, the St-Merri neighborhood around it declared as an *ilot insalubre*, an unhealthy enclave. The Marais was still run-down and the Fifteenth Arrondissement very industrial. Much of eastern Paris was impoverished, the Bastille and St-Antoine quarters hardly an arts district. Beyond the western border of the city, the La Defense complex stood little more than in a series of models. The familiar cranes and scaffolds of construction projects that have dominated the skyline since the real estate boom of the 1980s were little in evidence. A generation after its occupation, Paris was still recovering from the War. In its housing stock and the manner of dress, particularly of working people, reminders of the older way of life were still apparent. There were no supermarkets. Men wore moustaches and

There were no drapes. Wooden shutters provided darkness and privacy. I sat on the edge of the bed and waited for Denise to finish washing at the sink. The lamps from outside through the shutters made a pattern on the wall.

blue smocks. French culture dominated the media, and few Parisians spoke English or wished to.

We rode the Metro to Raspail, exited along the 1785 Wall of the Farmers General, though we did not know it, and walked the blocks to the Hotel Unic in the rue de Montparnasse where we had taken a room without a toilet for the extraordinary sum of fourteen dollars a night. If we wanted to shower, there were public baths down the street, a thing I wish I had done both for hygiene and pure experience. When we checked in I requested in my best French *"un lit matrimonial."* We gave the desk clerk our passports and she gave us an enormous key. I had never been in a room so small yet stuffed with furniture. An oracular sink stood in one corner and a table and chairs in the other. There were no drapes. Wooden shutters provided darkness and privacy. I sat on the edge of the bed and waited for Denise to finish washing at the sink. The lamps from outside through the shutters made a pattern on the wall. When the door opened and closed at the Breton restaurant across the street we could hear the accordion player whose notes sounded heartfelt but music long judged archaic. Naked and exhausted from our travels, we made love on the matrimonial bed and slept awhile, and being our age, made love again then slept.

The next morning, we walked down the rue de Rennes to La Hune bookstore in the boulevard St-Germaine where we imagined Jean Paul Sartre and Simone de Bouvoir, the ideal left-wing couple, shopped for the latest volumes of trenchant criticism. Passing the café Deux Magots, we saw them in all the middle-aged smoking faces. At La Hune I purchased the Gallimard edition of "Corps et Bien" by Robert Desnos whose poetry I recently read in the pamphlet Michael Benedikt published with Kayak Press.

On the strength of my ignorance I began cooking up some translations, one of which I published in *Agni* magazine—owing to the kindness of its editor and that hunger then for any poetry in translation, the *espirit* of the seventies.

LIKE A HAND AT THE MOMENT OF DEATH

Like a hand at the moment of death and shipwreck
it rises like the last beams of the setting sun.
so from all places your glances spring.
There is not enough time, there is not enough time
perhaps for me to see,
But the leaf that falls and the wheel that turns you
will say nothing is perpetual above the earth,
Except love,
And I want to be convinced.
Some salvage boats paint reddish colors,
Some storms vanish,

An old waltz sweeps away time and the wind
during slow intervals of sky.
Scenery.
Me, I don't envy the others who clasp what I desire
And kill the rooster's song.
Like a hand at the moment of death it shrinks, my
heart strains.
I will never cry because I know you.
I love my love too much to cry.
You will cry over my grave.
Or me over yours.
It won't be too late.
I'll lie. I'll say you were my mistress,
And then it really is so useless,
You and me, soon we will die.

My awkward grammar and stilted diction move me to this day. I sat at the table and field-marshalled my first major attack on the language How filled with illusion, this scene of myself seated by the window while Denise with her French name dozed on the bed. But like me, she was from Atlantic City not Paris, and when you grow up in such a place the boardwalk teaches you cleverness. Without a Surrealist Manifesto, it is possible to reinvent yourself.

Stuart Dischell is the author of Good Hope Road, *a National Poetry Series Selection, (Viking, 1993),* Evenings & Avenues *(Penguin, 1996),* Dig Safe *(Penguin, 2003), and* Backwards Days *(Penguin, 2007) and the chapbooks* Animate Earth *(Jeanne Duval Editions,1988) and* Touch Monkey *(Forklift, 2012). Dischell's poems have been published in* The Atlantic, Agni, The New Republic, Slate, Kenyon Review, *and anthologies including* Essential Poems, Hammer and Blaze, Pushcart Prize, *and* Garrison Keillor's Good Poems. *A recipient of awards from the NEA, the North Carolina Arts Council, and the John Simon Guggenheim Foundation, he is a the Class of 1952 Distinguished Professor in the MFA Program in Creative Writing at the University of North Carolina Greensboro.*

Jack Powers

The One Who Got Away

Andy Moreland practiced casting in the Continental Motors parking lot,
dropping his hand-tied fly between two used Saabs,
or on the windshield wiper of a Trans Am trade-in. His gold-buttoned

blue blazer lay folded beside him on a parked car. Across the pot-holed taxi lot,
trains pulled in and out of the station. The chatter of downtown
was drowned out by the steady line of trucks on 95. But the look on his face

said Montana. His casting and reeling were the opposite of the young guys
pacing at the BMW window next door double-crossing each other for Ups
and cursing each car-shopping hobbyist who kept money those bastards

had already spent on alimony, girlfriends and Italian suits. I marked time
learning crossword puzzle clues in the Saab showroom or dreaming up slogans
I knew we'd never use: "Continental Motors: A Touch of Class

in the Slums of Stamford" or "Come Celebrate Our 'We've Lived Longer
than Jesus Sale!'" As usual a girl had led me there—long gone now.
And inertia kept me there. And the girl who did the books who wrote me

long letters in the voice of imagined characters. We snuck out at lunch
to sit on the platform, watch the trains empty and fill as we invented names
for the faces framed in passing windows. When the 12:57 pulled out,

we headed back to the showroom: me to make money: her to count it.
I felt reeled into that life—imagining a small bungalow
on the quiet side of town, a little Jackie and a baby Lucille,

Saturday nights playing Scrabble around the space heater, Uncle Andy
teaching the kids to fish. Before I could tell her my plan, we went to dinner
at a dimly lit Chinese place, her sharp-chinned face hopeful and sincere

until we ran out of witty things to say—our store of Chinese names too limited,
the restaurant too empty, our loneliness suddenly too apparent.
By the time the night ended with a kiss in the used orange Saab

I took home each night, we'd already let each other go. For nine months
my life floated in that place. My painter and sculptor friends lived in cramped,
cockroached apartments in the West Village, my ambitious friends

marched off for law degrees or MBA's, my fellow stalled pals in town
drank too much and drove too fast searching for parties and Swedish au pairs.
Andy'd found a peace—or a truce—after a failed marriage or two, I suspect,

and the wisdom of AA. He'd never checked my made-up references
and tutored me with a gentle hand, his ruddy-faced laugh and, more and more,
by asking, "Why are you here?" I burrowed into the silences—waiting

for customers in those afternoons or in the moment after I laid out the deal
and the Up and I faced each other or in those mornings watching Andy
casting and reeling out the window, the flash of yellow fly, the glint of line

like a spider web in the sunlight. Not until a too-blonde forty-something
jangled the bells of the showroom door, sat down at my desk with a sigh
and wrote a check for a brown Saab for $500 more than the New Canaan dealer

a block from her home was I jostled awake. I promised to tear up the check
if she changed her mind, but we both knew she'd bought the car.
I pursed my lips, shook her hand, glanced at the lone cloudy pearl

laying against the dark freckles on her cleavage and realized
I was becoming the guys next door. Out the window, Andy pulled on his blazer,
tugged a centimeter of cuff out each wrist and winked at that poor Up,

flashing his sad, sincere smile. The bell jangled as he pushed through the door,
but I rushed by, out into the lot, waving my arms to chase her down,
change her mind or thank her, but she'd already merged into traffic

and disappeared under the train bridge into the heat and morning exhaust.

Dear Inspector #17

I hope this note finds you well. I'm sure the life of a shorts inspector in Macao is a difficult one. The pace, I imagine, is grueling and the heat of the factory sometimes more than you can bear and I must admit I'm not sure if inspectors are plucked from the best or it's just an entry level job off the crowded streets of your once quaint village. As an inspector myself (mortgage forms not khaki shorts) I appreciate what you do and believe you are driven to be the best inspector in the Far (or perhaps for you Near) East. However, the inner waist button on my double buttoned, unpleated casual short (model #AE 40667) has popped loose and the thread width and number seem to be the culprit. My ex-wife, of course, says it's my fault for "camping out at the buffet table," but I have worn this waist size since college without incident. You may not remember inspecting this particular pair of shorts. Sometimes I have to re-read the cost-to-down-payment ratio three times because I'm distracted by the cold rain here in Syracuse or the whine of the dusty heater that sounds like an old woman crying. I'm sure you have your own distractions in Macao—the rising steam after the monsoons, the call and response of tugboats in the harbor. Perhaps you left a sick child at home and your husband has never returned from the sea. We could never have children ourselves and I wonder if they just bring a different kind of sadness. Enclosed find the shorts and a stamped, addressed envelope. I have imagined your tan hands pulling each seam, your long finger checking the stitch on the hem and your dark eyes squinting to measure the weight of the fabric. Please re-sew my button and inspect my shorts again. Take your time, knowing I sit here in Syracuse picturing the wisps of ink-black hair falling from your bun, the beads of sweat that form above the brows you furrow in concentration and the tilt of your clavicles as you hold the pants up to the light. Please, Inspector #17, remember to sign the form and if time allows include a short note, so I know you are well and take a moment each day to know you are loved.

Peter Merkle's Eye

The Fronio brothers controlled the Boys Room
in seventh grade, greeting the unsuspecting
or desperate with an arm around the shoulder

and the occasional head flush—we didn't call them
swirlies then. Peter Merkel hung on the fringes,
knowing he'd be hassled most days,

forced to hand over his change and cigarettes,
and more and more often, the glass eye
replacing his original blue lost in a backyard accident.

He'd make a game of saying no until one of the boys
(often one of Peter's buddies in the outside world)
pinned his arms and threatened to take it out themselves.

Okay, okay, Peter'd say and slide a finger
under the eye and pop it out like a tiddly wink
catching it in the air. We were surprised every time

by the curved wedge like a sliver of oyster shell,
sand-worn and polished, the hazel streaks
whirling into the pale blue from the dark pupil

and the little red squiggles suggesting sleepless nights
until, embarrassed perhaps by our naïve wonder,
Billy tossed it in the urinal and flushed. We stared

as it stared back at us while struggling
to surf atop the whirlpool until Peter,
afraid it might slip down the drain, yelled

and reached out for the urinal. We pinned him
against the sink and stared as he swam in place
against the tide of our locked limbs.

I can see myself still in that drowning eye,
skinny and smooth-jawed, unwilling to tell them
to stop—even pinning Peter with my hip

—and staring back and forth at once
as if it was my own eye calling for a thrown line
—until someone, I hope it was me,

claimed to hear Mr. Loughran's voice in the hall
so Johnny scooped up the eye, tossed it to Peter
who paused only briefly before tossing it in his mouth

for a quick rinse and popping it back in place
as the Fronios wrapped an arm around his shoulders
and turned with broad smiles toward the door

as if Loughran would enter with a camera
eager to frame this ideal of friendship
for the front page of the yearbook.

Jack Powers won the 2012 Connecticut River Review Poetry Contest and was a finalist in both 2013 and 2014 for the Rattle Poetry Prize. His poems are forthcoming or have appeared in The Southern Review, Poet Lore, Barrow Street, Cortland Review, *and elsewhere. More poems at www.jack-powers13.com/poetry.*

K. J. Knoespel

Levitation in Glencoe, Illinois

One by one
we drifted
through the branches,
feet dangling
on the treetops.
Gravity let us go
as easily as slipping
from a sweater or shoes.
Curtis laughed and said
he could even see the lake,
and Celina wondered
if levitation like this
could happen in Atlanta?
Tina peddled faster,
her bike suspended.
Chadrak the dog leapt in the air,
and Helena's skirt fluttered in the twigs—
how she smiled
(she had been here before!)
Rönnog had us hold hands;
Steve headed for a summersault.
We floated with such grace.
And below us all,
having made their way
up the basement stairs,
the skeletons joined hands
as we circled in the sky.

Rönnog

In the falling dark
the lighted masts from the inlet
look like Christmas trees
as they cross the harbor.
Their wakes,
like memory,
curl and fill.

As I scan the shoreline,
I hear your voice.
You are asking your parents for ice cream.
You told me it was here
that you first dared to look
at the shadows under
the timbered bridge in the forest
and found your father
was Billy Goat Gruff.

Steve says you startled,
sat up
and, in your strong voice asked,
'What's the matter?'
the moment before you died.

Now you ask me
with your strong voice
if I can see through memories
that follow closer
than any dark silhouettes
falling against the sun.

Recipe and Melt Instructions
for 7 Tons Medium Grade Steel

Ingredients: Shop scrap, Steel plate, Lime, Manganese, Silicon, Alumi
num, Ferro-Manganese, Fero-Silicon, Pig Iron
Melt time: 1 hour, 19 minutes

Loading
Roof off
Carbon in
Nick away
Crane over
Warning
Crane Magnet
Scrap drop
Roof over
Roof closed
Swing
Heat Shield
To Furnace Door
Ear Plugs
Double Wax
Pushed deep

The scrap yard operator will prepare buckets of scrap according to the needs of the melter. Preparation of the charge bucket is an important operation, not only to ensure proper melt-in chemistry but also to ensure good melting conditions.

The first step in any tap-to-tap cycle is "charging" into the scrap. The roof and electrodes are raised and are swung to the side of the furnace to allow the scrap charging crane to move a full bucket of scrap into place over the furnace. The bucket bottom is usually a clam shell design—i.e. the bucket opens up by retracting two segments on the bottom of the bucket. The scrap falls into the furnace and the scrap crane removes the scrap bucket. The roof and electrodes swing back into place over the furnace. The roof is lowered and then the electrodes are lowered to strike an arc on the scrap.

Ignition

Power
Arch Flash
Bone Shock
Spark Shower
Ear Split

The long high-voltage arc maximizes the transfer of power to the scrap and a liquid pool of metal will form in the furnace hearth At the start of melting the arc is erratic and unstable. Wide swings in current are observed accompanied by rapid movement of the electrodes. As the furnace atmosphere heats up the arc stabilizes and once the molten pool is formed, the arc becomes quite stable and the average power input increases.

Test 1

Open Furnace
Door
Boiling Metal
Apron
Gloves
Goggles
Plunge
White Heat
Face away
No Skin
Burn
Rhythm
Arms swing
Ladle
In
Out
Cold Water
Bucket Hiss
Plug to
Lab
Capsule
Pneumatic Tube
Blow Furnace
With Oxygen
Watch boil
Add Aluminum

Once the final scrap charge is fully melted, flat bath conditions are reached. At this point, a bath temperature and sample will be taken. The analysis of the bath chemistry will allow the melter to determine the amount of oxygen to be blown during refining. At this point, the melter can also start to arrange for the bulk tap alloy additions to be made.

Test 2

Take Melt
Temp
Adjust to
Lab Report
Specs
Alloys
To ladle

Once the final scrap charge is fully melted, flat bath conditions are reached. At this point, a bath temperature and sample will be taken. The analysis of the bath chemistry will allow the melter to determine the amount of oxygen to be blown during refining. At this point, the melter can also start to arrange for the bulk tap alloy additions to be made.

Pour
Lift Electrodes
Lower Giant
Ladle Bucket
From Crane
Slag Tip
Crack Tap
Break Hole
Sun Slush
Then Sun
Pour
Bucket hoist
Rising
Sun

The furnace is tilted backwards and slag is poured out of the furnace through the slag door. Removal of the slag eliminates the possibility of phosphorus reversion.

Once the desired steel composition and temperature are achieved in the furnace, the tap-hole is opened, the furnace is tilted, and the steel pours into a ladle for transfer to the next batch operation.

Turn-Around
Lift Roof
Shovel
Patch Spout
With Sand
Climb in
Hot Furnace
Sledge Hammer
Crack Slag
Pack Burned
Walls with Sand

Furnace turn-around is the period following completion of tapping until the furnace is recharged for the next heat. During this period, the electrodes and roof are raised and the furnace lining is inspected for refractory damage. If necessary, repairs are made to the hearth, slag-line, tap-hole and spout. In the case of a bottom-tapping furnace, the taphole is filled with sand.

Excerpts: American Iron and Steel Institute Technical Report on *Electric Arc Furnace Steelmaking*

Wait Next Heat

Report from Melter's Helper #1
Wehr Steel Company, West Allis, Wisconsin
Summer 1968

K. J. Knoespel teaches at Georgia Tech where he participated in building Poetry@Tech. In addition to building courses and programs between disciplines in Atlanta, he has worked extensively with colleagues in Sweden, Russia, and France. He is a founding editor of Configurations: A Journal for Literature, Science, and Technology, *published by Johns Hopkins University Press and translates Swedish poetry.*

Cathy Allman

Pittsburgh as a Metaphor for My Father

My father was no stranger to factory life,
or the toxic bi-products spilled into the Allegheny
from making glass, steel, the river he swam in as a child,
but my father was a realist, no matter how much superstition
the stories in his childhood mass-produced.
My father, like his mother, like his father-figures
from the volunteer fire department next to their row house
had worked in the factory. He pushed large plates
of glass from the assembly line to where they would be cut,
then transported. If the glass dropped, there was blood.
Mindless, but he had to keep alert to the delicacy
of the manual labor. My father had his drinks at the bar
after his shift ended or at the fire department where the guys
would tell dirty stories, and he'd think of becoming a Cadillac salesman,
dream of wearing white shirts. Dad gave me a glamorous view
of fossil fuel when he sold for Eastern Coal. He explained to me
that without coal there would not be electricity, or steel. He explained
how coal was formed by prehistoric forest that had been buried by floods,
and time, and soil deposited over what used to be plant life
until enough time and heat converted trapped carbon
covered by peat bogs into coal. And I knew, that if coal stayed
in the ground long enough, for many millennium, un-mined,
the next step in the pressure transformation would be diamond.
He didn't just sell tonnage, one time my dad sold an abandoned mine,
he turned a profit off the unused. And Pittsburgh in those days was as dirty
as people used to think it was, smoke billowing so thick
that if you hung your white laundry on the clothesline out to dry
and didn't bring it in quickly the soot would stick, sheets weren't white
    anymore.

Unnecessary Darkness

I run before sunrise,
plodding through the fog
of unseasonable December warmth
and the hum of truck traffic on I-95.
I breathe in rhythm with the semi-hushed lapping
of the tide creeping higher into the salt marsh.

I pause on the stone bridge in pre-dawn's sepia.
The scent of wet mud tinged with decaying leaves lives here.
To the swan that floats here
night and light barely matter
because her food is underneath
the tidal surface.

My heart still races from running.
Heat rises like mist from my skin
under the gray sweatshirt.
For one silent second of between breaths
a notion of paradise almost forms, almost still,

but instead, I'm haunted with thoughts
about my 82-year-old father
and how he sees people who are not there.
He argues like a pit bull with my mother
about the figures that watch from outside,
says, "See the red tips of their cigarettes?
Close the hurricane shutters!"

She sits inside with him, shuttered
not watching the Florida sunset,
but simply eating meatloaf together
in the flickering TV light.

Between the Salt Marsh and the Sound

Leaves fall like unspoken prayers.
I shuffle past mold-spotted decay.

The path used to be rimmed with dropped
branches placed to point the way.

In earlier days there were signs to the water—
the sound on the other side.

If only I had strength enough
to swim to the horizon, into the sun-melt

and shimmer with those ripples the wind stirs.
If I could for one moment

push off the velvet shell-studded bottom,
break the surface, breathe again.

But in these woods there are tangled
prisons of roots,

and the stench of low tide, and rotted tree stumps
reek while rodents hide in holes.

I trudge through withered
amber and ash camouflage.

The snake calling, hissing.
The rats squeal. Dirt-coated tongues hum,

and teeth gnaw tunnels,
unearth gravel, turn the sand.

Six feet under, the left-behind world
of blue skies and springtime

lies—my lost life
dreaming beneath ice.

In this womb-cave of unbelief
my hardened mustard seed heart

bursts from its dried shell,
dissolves to fog

while gravity weaves
sky into vanishing point.

Virgin Mother's raised palms catch
rain from word-clouds

pouring without doubt,
writing on stones, Holy commands.

The forest floor breaks
the river splits.

I cross over the cracks.
Psalms scroll along slate.

Veins sing their
blood-wine chants

pant, push, pulse
seeds to trees.

Wind-breath rises,
undergrowth lifts

my lip-wings caught
between lungs and ribs

peel. Speak.
And just as when the Lord

reached into Adam,
I open,

born from dust
and bone.

Cathy Allman is a writer and educator living on Scott's Cove in Darien, Conecticut. Her work has ap-peared or is forthcoming in California Quarterly (CQ), Penman Review, Caveat Lector, Critical Pass Review, Edison Literary Review *and more.*

Nguyen Phan Que Mai

Tears of Quang Tri

After the last American soldiers
had left Vietnam
and grass had grown
scars onto bomb craters,
I took some foreign friends to Quang Tri,
once a fierce battlefield.

I was too young for war
to crawl under my skin
so when I sat with my friends
at a roadside café, sipping tea,
enjoying the now-green landscape,
I didn't know how to react
when a starkly naked
woman rushed towards us, howling.

Her ribs protruded like the bones
of a fish which had been skinned.
Her breasts swaying like long muop fruit,
and her womanly hair a black jungle.

I was too young to know
what to say when the woman
shouted for my foreign friends
to return her husband and children to her.

Stunned, we watched her fight against villagers
who snatched her arms and dragged her away from us.
"She's been crazy," the tea seller said.

"Her house was bombed.
Her husband and children…
she's been looking for them ever since."

My friends bent their heads.
"But the war was here forty-six years ago," I said.
"Some wounds can never heal," the tea seller shrugged.

And here I was, thinking green grass
could heal bomb craters into scars.

Nguyen Phan Que Mai is the author of four poetry collections and translator of six. Her literary awards include the Poetry of the Year 2010 Award from the Hanoi Writers Association; First Prize in the Poetry about Hanoi competition from Vietnam's Literature Newspaper and Hanoi Radio & Television; the Capital's Literature & Arts Award from the Hanoi Union of Literature & Arts Associations, among others. Her poems have been featured at major international poetry festivals including the First Asia-Pacific Poetry Festival; the Qinghai International Poetry Festival; and the International Poetry Festival of Medellin, Colombia. Que Mai is the Honorary Fellow of Writing at Hong Kong Baptist University. She is the first Vietnamese writer whose work is published as part of the prestigious Lannan Selection Translations Series. According to BOA Editions, The Secret of Hoa Sen, *Que Mai's first full-length U.S. publication, "shines with craft, art, and deeply felt humanity."*

Seth Michelson

Vencerémos: A Manifesto

—for Víctor Jara

They snapped
your fingers, one
by one, pain
exploding
from each knuckle,
till agony, only
agony
in your hand
was real and present.
Everything else
was echo: of bone
snapped
and crooked
fingers
in pain like snakes
set on fire
or butterflies
stitched alive
into a collector's
book, you
writhing there, Víctor
Jara, one more
body
amidst the many
being
whipped, hit, kicked
in Estadio Chile,

O civic cathedral,
pit of erasures,
where the sweaty
Comandante
rasped in spittle
hot into your ear,
Víctor, you'll
never again
strum or sing,
at least not here,
in this world,
as if a storm of slurs
and busted fingers
and crazy bullets
could kill a song.

Border Politics: A Manifesto

Brisenia Flores and her father, Raúl,
were shot to death in Arizona, killed
by racists who stalked the border
the way eels slither a river. Arizona
is O'odham, the region's
oldest known language, and means
"small spring," though the killers' interests
likely didn't include etymologies.
Instead they patrolled the small spring
with GPS, smartphones, and silver pistols,
using technology to contort
the ancient story of human migration.
To keep their word, to guard
their turf, they killed two US-born US citizens,
and to complete the mission, they shot
Brisenia's mom, Gina Gonzalez, too.
They called themselves Minutemen, though
no joke, they were led
by a woman, who preached freedom
the way Hitler professed love for German people, these
vigilantes who killed Brisenia and Raúl
and wounded Gina, too,
a young family vanished
in the orange flash of few, quick trigger pulls.
Gone, too, another lungful
of hope from the community
that, like you and me, learned the news
and felt pummeled by shame: What
violence is this? How to live

in its residue, our collective skin
stained with the smell of burnt tires,
of our homes going up in flames? Life
with the waft of our entrails roasted. Life
like the bafflement of cormorants
in a tanker's spill: oil
in our eyes and ears, oil
burning our throats, as we tip
and paddle in blind circles,
unable to see how we're each crying
and how we're each also somehow
a spectacular small spring.

Seth Michelson's most recent book of poetry is Eyes Like Broken Windows *(Press 53, 2012), winner of the poetry category of the 2013 International Book Awards. He also is the author of the chapbooks* House in a Hurricane *(Big Table Publishing, 2010),* Kaddish for My Unborn Son *(Pudding House Publications, 2009), and* Maestro of Brutal Splendor *(Jeanne Duval Editions, 2005). His poetry translations include the book* The Ghetto *(Point of Contact, 2011), which is his rendering of* El ghetto *(Sudamericana, 2003), by the internationally acclaimed Argentine poet Tamara Kamenszain, and* Roly Poly *(Toad Press, 2014), which is his translation of* Bicho Bola *(Yauguru, 2012), by the young Uruguayan poet Victoria Estol. His translation of the selected poetry of the renowned Indian poet Rati Saxena is forthcoming as* Dreaming in Another Land *(Kritya, 2014). He holds an M.F.A. in poetry and a Ph.D. in Comparative Literature, and he is a professor of the poetry of the Americas at Washington and Lee University. He welcomes contact through his website, www.sethmichelson.com.*

Esther Lee

If Jesus Inserted the Comma

> *Ain't no one gonna to turn me 'round.*
> —Big Star

We grew up on orange sugar & tragedy, nearly
dying on soda, creamsicles, lollipops, we weren't

kidding about birds spreading out for electricity.
We could have joked about their falling from trees,

how their moist bodies litter the sidewalk.
The next street over is where, merely manmade,

our hearts lived & forgot such stories hours
after the making: *Some days I miss the gruel.*

From left to right: a salesman who never makes
a sale, septic tanks brimming & squirming grains of rice!

In class, teachers distinguish your composing hand
from your plucking hand, instruct you to kiss

the paper rather than to bruise it. At home
you shank the baby shark in two—first

with handsaw (scissors wouldn't do), then with
a dull paring knife. All that tawdry flesh,

how easy, you think, for someone—anyone—
to gut you with syntax & connotation.

So, in defense of absentia—

for Vivian Maier

So, they say I am a problem with contradictory impulses.
So, yes, not a hobby.
So, apparently the word "so" appears before questions and before answers.
So, what to make of *self-portraits* and *street photographs* as gloves
       on separate hands. So, of you, yet not of you.
So, the doors ran past me, not the other way around.
So, what captivates is but a symptom we share.
So, my contact sheets dry as do sidewalks with their puddles.
So, you, too, like the unseemly.
So, like the man without an ear who holds the phone to the other side
      of his face, I knew better.
So, as for editing, who is the singular personality.
So, *How do you catch a cloud and pin it down?* was not my line. Neither were:
      How do you keep a wave upon the sand? nor *How do you hold a moonbeam in*
       your hand?
So, nowadays, according to some, yellowing newsprint frames my biography.
So, what gets in the way of bone is the meat.
So, you can ask Mr. Foster where all I have been.
So, yes, intentional. As much as mirrors in the streets.
So, notice how light betrays you—where you see the skull I see the window.
So, my use of "so" represents an alternate means to an end.
So, my interest in calves is the walking away.
So, again, whose eye had changed.

Noisiest Gaps

Tomorrow, they say, the roads will turn
to ice and ruin. No eating, no smoking
and soon—comedian warns—

libraries will enforce no
reading, no talking. Meanwhile:
our bars too loud, our cafés too quiet.

No surprise—it tastes remotely
like death, decibels thickening
air as we drink till witching

hour, when conversation turns
slushy, our nostalgia, passed
out after several rounds,

longing for earliest of eras.
Tomorrow, they say, an inch
of ice will decimate the trees.

This is when I will know
I am real: to hear the music before
the needle hits the vinyl, dance

every step before someone draws
the diagram—the grass will insist
on its slowest performance.

I've picked up a few things

after C.D. Wright

I've picked up a few things, I know if you want to see a forest, they say to separate each tree from its sapling and every sapling from its seed, and so on. I know the difference between fireworks and gunfire, that a man can drown on dry land. And I know sooner or later we'll get to talking. We'll move through tall grass and miss each other, continually, every morning, as if pushing through gold conveyors. But it's not that kind of story; it never was. How many times have I awoken to the sound of tearing paper. How many bony wings have I seen collapsed. We didn't know how to cup the water and keep it there. I know if I want to remember your face, to cut a paper towel roll in half; when I don't want to, throw away the broth. I wanted to show you I could step over the needle and never get it caught in my foot. It's like the day when you don't make your bed. When everything pulls up in a fistful of roots. I've picked up on how to walk past the pomegranates threatening descent. I've picked up on how to see your body everywhere, following me, a hue of blue the painter would spend the last of her money for. But that's not nothing—it's significant, otherwise you wouldn't want it.

Esther Lee has written Spit, *a poetry collection selected for the Elixir Press Poetry Prize (2011) and her chapbook,* The Blank Missives *(Trafficker Press, 2007). Her poems and articles have appeared or are forthcoming in* Ploughshares, Verse Daily, Salt Hill, Lantern Review, Good Foot, Swink, Hyphen, Born Magazine, *and elsewhere. A Kundiman fellow, she received her M.F.A. in Creative Writing from Indiana University where she served as Editor-in-Chief for* Indiana Review. *She has been awarded the Elinor Benedict Poetry Prize, the Utah Writer's Contest Award for Poetry (selected by Brenda Shaughnessy), the Snowcroft Prose Prize (selected by Susan Steinberg), as well as twice nominated for the Pushcart Prize. She recently received her Ph.D. in Creative Writing and Literature at the University of Utah. She teaches as an assistant professor at Agnes Scott College.*

Julie Innis

Monkey

For years growing up, I'd begged for a dog, what any boy wanted. Finally at fifty, I got my wish. Except that instead of a dog, I got a monkey. And not even a new monkey. A used monkey re-gifted to me by my mother. She'd received it from a man she was dating.

"Surprise!" her date said, thrusting the monkey forward when she opened the front door.

"Why thank you," she said as she took the monkey into her arms, dipping her head down as if she were about to smell its scalp but instead, much to my horror, planting a kiss square on its crown. This gesture was not lost on me; it was the way she had for many years sent me off to bed at night.

"Here you go," she said and passed me the monkey as if it were a bouquet of flowers in need of a vase. "Don't stay up too late," she called over her shoulder as she led her date down the hallway and into her bedroom, as she did with all of her dates, to spend the night ordering carry-out, listening to records, and doing god knows whatever else.

I just nodded as I made room on the couch next to me for the monkey before turning up the volume on the TV. I was used to her date-nights by now. My mother's agoraphobia kept her house-bound yet strangely restless, and while leaving the house for real dates was out of the question, finding men on the internet was not. It's like traveling, she claimed, without ever having to leave home.

To say that my mother was some kind of radical, a Patty Hearst held hostage by her own psyche, wouldn't be much of a stretch, as the men she lured to our home—social workers, pro bono lawyers, doctors without boundaries—were often men of great causes, some legitimate, most not. The monkey was a gift from her latest, the Environmentalist, she called him, an aging hippie with dreadlocks and a soul patch who, in addition to teaching school children about recycling, rescued primates from science labs. The monkey (a chimpanzee, the Environmentalist corrected me) was ten years old and underweight at only thirty pounds with a pelt grizzled gray (from stress, the Environmentalist explained) and worn through in spots, revealing leathery patches of skin. Above his left eye was a scar which prompted my mother to suggest the next morning over breakfast that we name him "*Serpico*, you know, like that cop movie?" a name I resented greatly as I was in the process of studying to retake my police exam.

On the verge of turning seventy, my mother had suddenly gained a fear of all things beyond the boundaries of her home, a raging internet addiction, and an all-consuming sex drive.

"This monkey is stolen property," I informed my mother after the Environmentalist left. "You have to return him."

"Pish posh," my mother said. "Besides, sons can't testify against their mothers in court."

"Oh yeah, what law is that?"

"The law of the womb," she said.

Her lawless nature aside, our living arrangement was less than ideal. On the verge of turning fifty, I'd lost my job, my house, and my wife. On the verge of turning seventy, my mother had suddenly gained a fear of all things beyond the boundaries of her home, a raging internet addiction, and an all-consuming sex drive. If it were not for the agoraphobia, I'd have gladly continued living out of a room at the Hotel 6. But she needed someone to pick up her groceries and bring in her mail.

Most nights that my mother had her boyfriends over, I patrolled the streets in an old police car, Monkey safety-belted into the passenger seat. Monkey and I'd drive our rounds for hours, timing it so we'd get home well after my mother had turned off the lights and gone to sleep.

I liked the quiet of these drives, the low crackle of the police scanner and the slight high-pitched whistle Monkey's nose made when he breathed. Deviated septum, I figured and wondered if it had always been that way or was a result of his time in the lab. Was it possible that monkeys in the wild have deviated septums, I wondered and if so, wouldn't it alert tigers and other predators to their location? I'd always been a big fan of nature shows, but these sorts of practical concerns never seemed to be addressed. Like why Monkey was so transfixed by the scanner—its lights, its sounds, its knobs, and, most of all, its hand-held microphone? No matter how often I told him not to, he couldn't seem to keep from playing with the curled plastic cord of the scanner's microphone, pulling it out as far as it could go before letting it snap

I liked the quiet of these drives, the low crackle of the police scanner and the slight high-pitched whistle Monkey's nose made when he breathed. Deviated septum, I figured [...]

back into place. Was this animal instinct, natural primate curiosity, or was he just trying to piss me off?

"Cut it out," I had to tell him more than once and based on the mischievous gleam in his eyes, I knew he'd been around humans long enough to understand me perfectly. "This scanner was expensive," I added, feeling a little guilty for yelling, as I fit the mouthpiece carefully back into place and retuned the dials.

Most nights the scanner broadcasted petty stuff—vandalism, kids doing doughnuts in a parking lot or batting practice on a string of mailboxes, firecrackers thrown off garage roofs—these we ignored. Ignored too were the domestic disturbances, mainly on the weekends past whatever hour husbands had told their wives they'd be home. "I'm not too keen on checking out those scenes," I explained to Monkey once.

"For personal reasons," I felt the need to add. Like he'd understand?

Some nights though we hit the jackpot—a mugging, a fender-bender, a suspected break-in, and off we'd go, taking the fastest route I could find through the back streets, angling our car up to the curb in time to watch the sweep of some cop's MagLite as he checked the perimeter, or to watch as a cop took notes from eyewitnesses as wrecked cars sat steaming in the middle of intersections and drivers and passengers were loaded into waiting ambulances. "Minor injuries, it looks like," I was quick to reassure Monkey. He'd been through enough trauma in his life, I knew, and I was a little conflicted about exposing him to more.

Still, I couldn't help but notice that he watched these scenes with the same intensity and posture as I did, pitched forward in his seat, leathery fingers and opposable thumbs braced against the dashboard as he peered through the windshield. Was it just his natural propensity for mimicry or something more? These were the thoughts that kept me awake long after we'd returned to the house and I'd tucked Monkey into his little bed for the night.

I'd bought the car at a police auction. A decommissioned Crown Vic out of a line-up of flashier models—a black Lexus with blacker tinted windows, a souped-up red Honda Civic, a safety-yellow Hummer. "Drug dealers and their cars," my friend Charlie explained. He'd been on the force five years and had more than once offered to help me study for the exam. I've known Charlie my whole life. He'd always tested well.

"Here she is, good condition," he said, rapping his knuckles on the Vic's hood. The Vic was stripped of its siren and township emblems and covered in a thin film of dirt, its front-end slightly off kilter the way a woman cocks her hip. "Car chase. Cracked chassis. A little body work, a couple of bolts, and she's good as new," Charlie said. The force was switching over to hybrids. "Green initiative. Probably make us use hand crank radios, ray guns. Get it? Like solar-powered, by the sun's rays?"

Charlie may have tested well, but he'd always been a complete nerd. Better suited for Best Buy blues than I was. The whole thing made my stomach hurt.

"Under-employed," my mother said when one of her boyfriends asked me what I did.

"Part-timer," I quickly corrected her. "Career-changer," I added.

"Changing into what?" the boyfriend asked.

"It's evolving," I said at the same time my mother said "Deputy Dog."

In my spare time, I fixed up the Vic. Charlie was right, she drove like a dream and for my birthday that year, my mother surprised me with the police scanner.

"Mom, I think this is illegal," I told her.

"Nothing is illegal," she told me.

Hers was an unbreakable logic.

The Pro-bono Lawyer had found it for her on eBay, installed it, showed me how to tune the dials. "You like playing cops and robbers, eh?" he said, clapping me on the shoulder as he handed back my car keys. Avuncular, father-like, even though the most he outpaced me by was ten years, maybe a little less.

"Mom," I told her once. "It pains me to say this, but look at these guys. They're too young for you. Can't you at least try to be a little more age-appropriate?"

She shook her head sadly. "Son, son. By now, I'd think you'd know women better than you do."

It was because of Monkey's dexterity with door knobs that my mother insisted I start taking him with me at night. "He's been scarred enough," she said, winking, scarring me in the process by her implication.

Between my mother and the monkey, I never got any privacy. I was in the habit of taking a shower before rounds to keep myself alert and damn it if Monkey couldn't give me a minute's peace. He liked to bury his face in my bath towel, suck toothpaste straight from the tube, trace lines in the steam on the mirror. He pissed me off, really. Sometimes I'd look at the lines on the mirror and imagine Monkey was trying to communicate with me. My ex always complained I never looked for signs and now that was all I did.

Crazy. Like Monkey had something to tell me that I hadn't already heard?

I wanted us to be buddies like you see in those cop shows, but there were nights when Monkey screwed around too much, constantly fiddling with the radio dials, pulling the mic to the end of its cord before letting it clatter back against the dashboard and I'd have to cut rounds short, skipping the diner, skipping the drive-bys. "God damn it Monkey. Can't you be serious for once," I'd snap.

I often wondered where he'd been before the laboratory. A zoo? A circus? The jungle? Monkey seemed to lack serious street smarts, so I doubted he'd ever known the leafy heights and mossy depths of any natural habitat. Still there were times when he seemed so homesick, the way he slumped in his seat, resting his chin against the seatbelt strap, tugging at the corners of his mouth. I felt so sorry for him, I'd unbuckle his seatbelt and let him climb up on my shoulders and groom me while I drove, the round pads of his fingers soft against my skull. I'd seen this once on a nature show and it never failed to cheer Monkey up.

Most nights though, Monkey was great company and midway through our rounds, we'd stop at the diner off Rt. 4, open all night, clean, bright. I'd get a coffee and Monkey'd get a fruit plate with a side of straws. I taught him how to shimmy off the paper wrapper from his straw so that it resembled a worm. Then, with just the lightest touch of water, he could make the wrapper wriggle and writhe. He got really good at it, focused, worked the wrapper carefully between his index finger and thumb, angled his straw into his water glass, experimenting until he got the perfect water to paper ratio.

Living with an agoraphobic mother and a monkey was more of a handicap than I could reasonably overcome, I'd long ago accepted.

"Cool," the waitress said each time. She was pretty enough; a blue-eyed blonde with dark roots that made me think if she gave it enough time, a whole different woman would grow out of her, something secretly more my type—raven-haired, dark-eyed, dangerous. Suzie was young and sunny. She liked to tease me, called Monkey my son, held out bananas to him, laughing when his rubbery lips flapped together against her palm. "It tickles," she giggled. She wasn't the sharpest girl I'd ever met, but I figured this to be an advantage. Living with an agoraphobic mother and a monkey was more of a handicap than I could reasonably overcome, I'd long ago accepted. Still, when Suzie wasn't looking, I'd check myself out in the reflection of the diner's plate-glass windows, doing what I could to fluff my thinning hair and suck in my gut.

"You have a lovely personality," my mother liked to say. "Accentuate the positive for a change. Don't be such a quitter."

I took my mother's advice and tried to work with what I had. I forced myself to show my teeth when I smiled and listened carefully, nodding along, as Suzie told me about her shift, what customers had ordered, what they'd sent back, who tipped and who stiffed. One time I asked if I could borrow her name tag. "I'm teaching Monkey how to read," I told her as she dropped her tag into my hand, her fingernails tickling briefly against my damp palm. I threw my arm around Monkey, avuncular-like, and pulled him close, directing his attention to her name tag as I sounded out her name slowly. "Suz...ie," I said, pointing at the tag and then at Suzie, Monkey's head turning to follow my hand. He suddenly laughed and clapped his hands together which made Suzie giggle and clap back with him.

"You're cute," she said, but I couldn't tell which one of us she meant and before I could think to ask her to clarify, a four-top came in and she rushed off to take their order.

"We should probably get going," I told Monkey when it became clear Suzie wasn't in any hurry to come back around to check on us. As he slid out from the booth, Monkey reached for my hand and gave it a little squeeze, as if to say "hey, you did your best." I nodded down at him and made sure to smile as I settled the bill before circling back to our table, as I always did, to leave a big tip.

"Why don't you give him a name?" my mother complained. "Bobo, Jimmy, George. Calling him Monkey makes it seem like you lack imagination."

So nights when there was nothing coming through on the scanner, I tried out names for size. Buddy, Hector, Mr. T, but none of them fit as well as "Monkey" did. Though when Monkey got a certain look on his face, eyes narrowed, brow furrowed, the tip of his tongue jutting out from the corner of his mouth, he looked so much like my kid brother, Bill, that I wondered if reincarnation was possible, if somehow Bill's soul had landed in this monkey who just so happened to end up at our house in the arms of my mother's environmental terrorist lover. Stranger things have happened, I told myself, and though I was never able to think of any convincing examples, I was pretty sure there must be. It was a big world and, admittedly, my experience of it only extended so far.

It took me a while to time it just right so that Suzie was almost at the end of her shift, close enough for me to offer, casually, one night, "Need a ride?"

She looked out through those big plate-glass windows to where I gestured. "Is that an old police car?"

"Yeah," I nodded.

"No fucking way," she said. "I've seen the inside of enough of those in my time."

"I'm not really a cop," I hurried to explain. "I can't even pass the entrance exam. It's just a car I bought, like a hobby."

"Yeah, sorry, I've heard that before," she said, chucking Monkey a couple times under his chin before turning away.

The fry cook told me later that the diner was part of a work-release program. "You know, for the women's prison? She hates cops. Even wannabes like you."

The way he said it, I knew he didn't mean to offend. All guys have game and mine just so happened to be in the form of a decommissioned Crown Vic. So I let the insult slide, and though we kept stopping off at the diner from time to time, Suzie never really warmed back up to me. She was nice enough about it, always calling out a "Hello Buddy" to which Monkey would respond by clapping and turning in his seat while I waved back, reminding myself to accentuate the positive and to smile with all my teeth. Honestly though, after a couple times of this, I started to suspect that the whole world was full of sin and I was on the wrong side of the Law to ever hope to partake in it.

He picked the lock on the front door, then walked down the hall in his sock feet to the bedroom where he caught my mother in full throes with the Banker, the Doctor or maybe it was the Lawyer.

I knew it wouldn't last. I should've steeled my heart better against what I knew would be the outcome. My mother was not suited for monogamy, it wasn't in her nature, and one night while I was out on rounds, the Environmentalist broke into the house. He'd sensed something was up and drew on his extensive training in stealth eco-terrorism to get to the bottom of his suspicions. He picked the lock on the front door, then walked down the hall in his sock feet to the bedroom where he caught my mother in full throes with the Banker, the Doctor or maybe it was the Lawyer. Either way, the Environmentalist was not so much a "Live and Let Live" kind of guy as he was a jealous and spiteful one.

"But Monkey was a gift," my mother cried later when he came for his things. I stood in the hallway outside my mother's bedroom and Monkey scampered up to my shoulder, weaving his fingers tightly around my neck. It hurt, but nothing like how it felt when the Environmentalist turned to me.

"The chimp goes with me," he said.

"Do something," my mother yelled at me as I tried to remember if possession was nine-tenths of the Law or if there was some statute that would allow Monkey to remain in my custody until the courts were able to sort things out.

But the most I was able to get out was "Please, no." It was not my finest moment, though it is one I've replayed many times since: the Environmentalist prying Monkey's hands from around my neck, Monkey's sad face over the Environmentalist's shoulder, his tongue jutting out from the side of his mouth, his chin dropped down to the seatbelt as the Environmentalist backed out of our driveway and drove away.

For weeks after that, we didn't speak, my mother and I. She didn't have any men over and I didn't drive my rounds. "I talked to the Environmentalist," she finally told me one night. I didn't bother to turn the TV down, but I listened. Some kind of work release program. They were taking Monkey to a jungle somewhere. Madagascar, or maybe it was Indonesia, she wasn't sure.

"That's good, right?" she said, her voice cracking slightly.

I just nodded and shrugged.

I didn't explain to her that Monkey wasn't suited for that world, that he lacked street smarts and I worried that at night he'd be afraid, the sounds of tigers below, their ears pitched toward that little whistling noise his nose made when he breathed. I think of Monkey still and hope he's making out okay. Sometimes late at night when I'm on rounds, I pull the scanner's microphone all the way out to its end and then I just let it go.

Julie Innis is the author of Three Squares a Day with Occasional Torture. *Her stories and essays have been widely published and have received several awards and mentions, including, most recently, a Notable Story designation by the* Best American Nonrequired Reading *series, edited by Dave Eggers.*

Allison Joseph

The Pervert's Shoe

is as glassy and shiny
as retail, crisp as money
new-minted by forgers

wise in the stink
of nightly ink. He has two,
you know, a special

pair silent over parquet
floors and parking lots,
able to burnish

the grime-streaked
corridors of hospitals.
He can find that trap

door you're sure your
landlord nailed shut,
surreptiously unscrewing

your screens off
their hinges, whispering
his way through

your sleep-damp rooms,
until his palm hovers
over your lips, hand

falling ceaselessly
down the second
you awaken to scream.

Letter to My Twelve-Year-Old Self

So roughly beautiful, so sad-sack
skinny and wrong-way awkward,
you fear everything and anything,

all elbows and acne, stutter-thick
glasses and heat-rash haloes,
stubble of new hair in old

places. No diva, princess, model,
you finger holes in derelict
denim, pray aloud to the grand

god of puberty to bless you
with a desired body, breasts
high atop your chest, curves

haunting hips and the plain
blank spaces of your limbs.
You can't see anything but

your own ugly—braceface teeth,
church-knob knees, untamed hair
no chemical can fix. And I could

be kind, tell you one day you'll
be married, needed, safe,
you'll be valued for that mind

and that wit, all the physical
ceasing to matter, never a
tantrum in a clothing store,

never a diatribe after another
cover, glorious in celebrity Photoshop,
lands in your lap, in your mail.

But this is what you must know—
there will be fat days, bloat days,
sweat stains, indescribable hairs

in every wrong niche, will be
riches of embarrassments,
rip-offs of hormones, rigors

of weeks where everything
you touch gains the power
to make you that much smaller.

There will be limbs you'll lust for,
legs that will scurry away
just as you confess, you left

with all that ache and nowhere
to shove it. Your body will feel
like a house, a store, vacant lot

where carjackers abandon
burnt-out wrecks. But it's still
your body—fat, thin, old, young,

indifferent, in pain or bliss.
Those doubt-bitten lips? Yours.
Those glands spitting out drama?

Those passion plays of breath?
All yours. I could try to tell
you different, but that would

make us both liars, and no one needs
another liar, not you—caged-tooth warbler,
not me—middle-aged prophet.

Allison Joseph's most recent book of poems, My Father's Kites, *was published by Steel Toe Books.*
Poems have appeared or are forthcoming in North American Review, Spoon River Poetry Review,
Sou'wester, TAB: The Journal of Poetry and Poetics *and* Southern Indiana Review.

Ross Peters

The Good Brother

When I looked in the mirror,
I could always find you, but now
You have disappeared from the surface.
You've moved deeper in.

To reach you I would have
To cut my knuckle on the breaking glass,
Still falling as I pull away my fist.

When I was young, I could have
Stolen something, wrecked something.
I could have picked the wrong battle,
I could have brought a sharp wit to a knife fight.

I went shin deep in the wash of bigger mistakes,
But you went all the way in.
You were nothing if not committed.

And now I see you, and now we speak.
Our conversation is no longer long—
Its muscles have atrophied
Back into an evasive, scrawny prepubescence.
We have become unrecognizable.

On the phone you sound young,
But you are not—
You have always been part of an old story,
And now you have grown into its dust-full skin.
It is the only place we are together.

Our sadness is the sadness of halves—

Put us together and we are diminished.
We were never something as simple as addition.
We multiply each other,
And are become cartoons.

I am the good brother
And I married the girl,

But you are the one she loved.

A native of Richmond, Virginia, Ross teaches English and serves as Head of Upper School at The Westminster Schools in Atlanta, Georgia. His interests include hiking in the Blue Ridge Mountains, travel, and somewhat awkward guitar picking. He is married to Katie, a teacher at Oglethorpe University, and they have a daughter, Eleanor. The Peters also have a bright red Australian terrier named Mic who has a strangely endearing overbite. Peters is currently working on a collection of poetry entitled, The Kiln.

Jeffrey McDaniel

Moore, Moore, Moore

My name is Sean Moore. If my name were Sean Lester, or Sean Lesko, even Sean Leschuk, I wouldn't be, I wouldn't forever be leaping off the precipice of *yes* into the great unknown, flapping my tattooed wings through the belly of the night. Recklessness wouldn't lean towards me with her green, go-for-it eyes, her red mouth hanging open just an inch, as she holds out a pair of gold dice. In some other world, I am Sean Lester, conceived at a decent hour, looking at Marnie Jones, my girlfriend of three years, next to me at the Fox and Hounds bar in Washington DC. In some other world, I am saying *not tonight* to Recklessness and paying the bartender and calling it a night. But that is not this world. In this world, I am Sean Moore, More, More. In this world, I want it now, now, now. In this world, it's April 7th 1992. I'm twenty-four years old. Marnie goes to the bathroom and makes the mistake of leaving me alone at the table with her friend, Amir, who has just flown in from England. In this world, I am leaning forward, taking the dice from Recklessness' soft hand.

"So Marnie has work in the morning and needs to go home. Do you want to call it a night, or keep the party train rolling?" I stare into Amir's dark eyes, set deep in his olive face, and try to gauge how far up the skirt of Debauchery he's willing to go. I slam back the amber liquid at the bottom of my Jack and Ginger. Amir and Marnie did coke together in England, yet he looks so straight-laced in his corduroy pants and stylish sweater and fall jacket, kind of like a very tan version of Gene Wilder. I can tell by his square teeth that the sex that produced him featured short, quick thrusts, like a roofer nail-gunning shingles into place. I haven't done hard drugs in almost a month, just around the clock bong hits and blasts of booze, but now the little mouth in my bloodstream is begging for a treat.

"Fear and loathing, mate," Amir says, his eyes glittering like spider shells.

Marnie maneuvers back from the bathroom, through the maze of tightly packed tables. For the first six months of our relationship we were true love, but the love has been intense, but flickering ever since. Her body sways more when she has a few drinks in her, giving her boobs a little more swing. Marnie is one of those rare creatures who was produced by healthy copulation, as though her parents were conscious of what they were doing when they made her, like each squeeze, each touch, corresponded to an emotion. She's walking proof that "making love" is possible, that sex can be four-dimensional. "You guys ready," she asks. Marnie is a sweet girl and probably deserves better than me. When Matt, my first poetry teacher, met her in college, the first thing that he said to her was that she had more class in her little finger than I had in my whole body, which kind of pissed me off. "I think Amir and I are gonna stay out a little longer," I say, as we exit the Fox and Hound, the classiest dive bar in DC.

"Just don't come home too late, Sean." Marnie's smile flattens out. "Remember—it's his first night in America." Marnie met Amir during her junior year abroad in Oxford and had some kind of romance with his best friend, Jim, the son of Lord Brent, the fifth richest man in Great Britain. I tell her not to worry. It's April 7th, 1992. I'm a graduate student in creative writing, with no classes the next day. Marnie slips off in a cab. A bear-shaped man approaches, holding a sketchpad, his eyes burning in his forehead like hot coals. "I'll draw your portrait for a dollar," he says, scribbling as he walks. "Just trying to get something to eat." I laugh: get-a-bite-to-eat panhandlers have been off the street for hours. "I'll sketch you for a dollar," he says, undeterred. He's the result of slow, but strenuous sex, where the participants were locked in a deep, silent groove, rocking back and forth in a cradle of *yeah*.

"Do me, Artisto," Amir laughs.

"Yeah, you should do a before and after," I say. "Before the rock, and after the rock." I make my face all bug-eyed. Crack is not my drug of choice. In fact, if all the hard drugs in the world were laid out on a table buffet-style, crack would be the last I'd choose. But we're in DC, and the only drug you can cop on the street is crack, a drug so insidious its name is a verb.

"I know where to get the rock," Artisto says matter-of-factly.

"You know where to get the rock?" I ask, no longer laughing. Artisto nods. Tiny marbles of sweat shine on his dark forehead in the weary streetlamp. I give Amir a you-cool-with-that glance.

"Fear and loathing, mate," Amir smiles.

We turn the corner, pile into my gray T-Bird: me and Amir in front, Artisto in the back. It feels like the beginning of a joke: *a white guy, an Indian guy, and a black guy get in a car*, but I don't know what the punch line is.

"Take a right here," Artisto commands. "Down this alley. Stop. Here." We're on the outskirts of upscale Dupont Circle. I have two hundred bucks in my wallet. I only give Artisto forty. That way if he rips us off and doesn't return, our losses will be minimal. And as long as he thinks I still have money, he has an incentive to return. Ten minutes later he's back with several juicy nuggets. He stuffs a rock in a glass pipe and passes it to me. I hit it with a flame. A taste like burnt cotton candy fills my mouth. Some drugs take their time wading through your bloodstream, like a drowsy herd of buffalo, but crack ricochets through you, like a crack rippling through a windshield. One or two hits are enough to get you skyscraper high, but the rub is that the high begins to lose its platinum sheen in minutes, so you keep toking to keep the high rolling. I take another hit. My heart starts kicking like a poorly-dubbed Kung Fu movie. The steering wheel an anchor in my grip.

We turn the corner, pile into my gray T-Bird: me and Amir in front, Artisto in the back. It feels like the beginning of a joke: *a white guy, an Indian guy, and a black guy get in a car*, but I don't know what the punch line is.

One hundred-and-forty dollars later, I feel trapped in either the second or fourth dimension. Each red light I encounter is a complex negotiation. How do people know when to press the brakes, I wonder. I feel like a golfer with a putter, approximating the car to a halt. Finally I can't take it anymore. I pull over, the engine idling. "Here, Amir, you drive."

"But I don't know how to drive an automatic, mate. In England, we only have stick."

"I don't care, man. Figure it out, bro." I step out. Amir slides over. In the backseat, Artisto is wedging the steel tip of a screwdriver into the crack pipe's basin, trying to conjure up one more puff, his eyes bulging. Amir is an even worse driver than me. He putt-putt stops forty feet before the red light but I don't care; it's not my problem. Circling between Dupont Circle, Mount Pleasant and the U Street Corridor, we haven't seen a single cop car all night. It's as if we have anti-cop radar, which is a good thing, because the cops would probably be suspicious of an older black guy being charioted around the Nation's Capital at three in the morning by a guy in his mid-twenties with olive-skin and a white boy with ill-kept dreads in a banged-up T-bird.

Artisto tilts his head up from the pipe and snaps, "Come on, drive right, boy." He has the authoritative tone of a manager on a loading dock. I wonder what Artisto did in life before it came to midnight panhandling and sketching drunks for drug money. I slide a Public Enemy cassette into the tape deck; the song repeats the phrase: *please, oh please, oh please/just give me just one more hit.* It's a persona rap in the voice of a crack head, and the booming bass thump is a monotonous, haunting drone that superbly captures the paranoid basehead's brainscape, like the mind is a dog leashed to a pole, chasing its own tail in circles until it's one big blur. We make fun of dogs for pursuing their own tails, for barking at their own shadows, but is it really that much different with us humans? When you boil it all down, isn't what we chase through life really our self? Business people work so hard making that scrilla, hunting those Benjamins—but isn't part of the motivation the notion that one day we might receive a dollar bill with our own picture on it, so we can know once and for all that we are ok? I rewind the *please, oh please, oh please* song and crank it. I feel like a mirror staring into a mirror—Here I am jonesing for a hit of crack, listening to a song about someone jonesing for a hit of crack. I am a rock hitting a still lake and rippling outward.

> # We make fun of dogs for pursuing their own tails, for barking at their own shadows, but is it really that much different with us humans?

"Yo, turn this shit off!" Artisto bellows from the backseat. I quickly acquiesce, because even though it's my car and my money, Artisto is clearly in charge of this operation. "I hate fucking rap music," he snaps. "Don't you have any jazz?" I don't, so I just turn the stereo off, and we each listen to the static blaring in our private heads. The numerals on the dashboard's digital clock make no sense; their reference point has become unhinged. The digital numbers are markings from some remote language. Even the sky, still dark, but now with a hint of blue injected into its blackness, means nothing.

An hour later, Artisto emerges from crackhouse number five, a woman on his arm. They climb into the backseat. The woman isn't a prostitute, not in the traditional sense anyway. She isn't wearing make-up, or dressed fancy, just the clothes one might wear to the corner store, if one were thirsty late at night.

We drive around for a couple minutes, then Artisto commands us to park at the end of an alleyway, says he has to *take care of some business*. He and the woman disappear. It is officially light out now. I stare out the smudged windshield. We are across the street from an elementary school. Freshly scrubbed brown faces bubble across the schoolyard, with their knapsacks, into the building. I feel like a piece of trash that's oozed into their neighborhood, a long-haired phony who writes poetry, just another honkie dirtball in a car holding a crack pipe to his lips, like one of the devil's chicken bones.

"Fear and loathing," Amir says with a purple smile.

Artisto slides back into the car, alone. "Let's go downtown. I got work to do." I close my eyes for a second. When I open them, we're downtown: a spread of large-windowed government office buildings planted squarely, like boxes, on a wide boulevard.

"You come along," Artisto says, pointing at me. Amir curls up in the front seat. I follow Artisto, who grips a sketchpad in one hand, and a marker in the other. The seven a.m. sidewalks brim to life with government people uniformed in bland-colored slacks and buttoned-up shirts. Artisto hustles up beside a white guy. "Want to have your portrait done, sir?" The white guy waves him off with barely a glance. "Come on, hurry up," Artisto snaps at me. He has two voices, just like my mom: the friendly, let-me-please-you voice for the people he wants to impress, and the bossy voice reserved for me, his bumbling assistant. Maybe it gives him a morsel of prestige to have a white guy as "his assistant," even though I'm not even holding a pen or paper, I'm just standing there, squirming under the dismissive eyes of the white guys in numb-colored suits. Mostly they stare through us, but every now and then a gaze is aimed at me, a direct kick to the ribs. A gaze that says: *what the hell are you doing out here?*

"Hey, Artisto," I finally say, "let's get out of here, man. I've got twenty more bucks."

We drive to crackhouse number six. Artisto hops out. Amir and I wait in the car for about ten minutes, but Artisto doesn't come out, so, at 8:20 a.m., eight hours after saying bye to Marnie, we officially call it a night.

I slide my key in Marnie's door and whisper: "Hey, Amir, don't say anything about what we did. I mean, you can say we were doing coke. But don't mention the crack. Or Artisto. Definitely not Artisto."

"No problem, mate. Fear and loathing."

We open the door. Marnie is fully dressed, smoothing on make-up and towel drying her hair at the same time. She looks astonishingly professional, like she could interact with the people we'd just been trying to hustle on the street. "Where the hell have you been? I almost called the police."

"We just had a late night," I say.

"It was brilliant, Marnie," Amir jumps in. "We picked up this homeless guy. He was an artist. We went to crackhouses. It was top-shelf."

"What?!" You took him to a crackhouse?! It's his first night in America!"

"No, no. We were just outside. We didn't go in," I reassure her.

"I can't deal with this now. I'm late for work," Marnie says, pushing out the door.

I crawl into Marnie's bed, close my eyes, and clench my jaw, my teeth grinding like the wheels of the train rolling me towards sleep.

Jeffrey McDaniel is the author of five books of poetry, most recently Chapel of Inadvertent Joy *(University of Pittsburgh Press, 2013). Other books include* The Endarkenment *(Pittsburgh, 2008),* The Splinter Factory *(Manic D, 2002),* The Forgiveness Parade *(Manic D Press, 1998), and* Alibi School *(Manic D, 1995). His poems have appeared in numerous journals and anthologies, including* Best American Poetry *(1994 and 2010). A recipient of an NEA Fellowship, he teaches at Sarah Lawrence College and lives in the Hudson Valley.*

John Mahnke

Side Effects

My side effects have side effects.
Requiring their own medicines, imaging and doctors,
Transfusions, immune system collapses and ER admissions.
Or are those underlying conditions?
With memory mostly more tired static
And concentration mere flickering, who knows.
Blood added for hemoglobin plunges, subtracted for tests.
Multiplication and division supplied by
Insurance company flamenco stalling.
Blood the constant preoccupation.
If you had to pick a cancer,
This varietal of leukemia said to be best.
Unless it mutates to sweep you up.
Good poison for bad cells
And all the good cells in the way.
Sparks from the banked
Fire in the marrow landing
On the blood till it blazes.
Most people at the clinic with worse prognoses,
All ages, faiths, nations, survival rates.
RC Priests with attending nuns
Beside Hasidic Rabbis with attentive sons.
And plenty of women.
Beyond blood cancer corner
A department here for every part of the body,
Specialists for each of those cancers.
Stunning how many.
The surprise wears off.
No more becoming.
It's time to be.

Economy of Design

Pigeons
beak tips joined
swirl a circle
and part
one trailing the other,
impossible
grace for this species.

Usually, step, bobblehead forward, peck,
step, bobblehead back,
twitch and sometimes coo, economy
of design, nothing extra for walking.

Squirrel's sudden high strung
stopping starting
misaligned with time,
half random as if
shortcuts were made
in the engine.
Enough for its purpose.
But what's the plan?

And what can't we have? What
don't we need beyond our purpose
that another being may have and use
perhaps to run the heavens or understand?
Or can we go beyond, is that the design?

Pidgin metaphysics
vouchsafed to mortals can't decide,
with those crazy squirrels leaping into the feeder,
where it's written in birdseed
the short answer and the long.

John Mahnke's recent work has appeared in Cloudbank *and* The Cortland Review. *His latest collection of poems, as yet unpublished, is called* Witness of Last Resort. *He works as a consultant on documentation projects for government and business.*

Jillian Weise

I had a little cash

I had a little cash and I was going to buy a little gun
but they said, No, no, you mustn't
They are in The Club of Ten Toes and Anti-Establishment
They said, Believe in the police
We believe in the police
All you have to do is call them
They come running, running
I had a little cash to buy a gun
but they said, Why would you do that
Who are you to do that
We do not do that with our money
I want to raise a goat in a field
I want to protect the goat from a mountain lion
If it's about animals, then may I buy a gun for it?
I had the cash to buy the gun
but they said, You can't you're a poet
Poets don't buy guns
So I dressed with my empty leather holster
(in truth I was thinking of some poets
just South of here who go shooting—
I know I am not alone), so I wore my holster
over my blue jeans and said to them,
What do you want me to do
Should I wait for something fatal to happen
Oh, you want me to run
Should I ask the attacker to give me a head start
Ask him to count to twenty before he chases me
You want me to gun-less run leg-less across a field
Are you trying to get me killed

I had a little cash so I bought the gun
but don't tell anyone
I'd hate to be alive and ostracized

Jillian Weise's recent collection, The Book of Goodbyes *(BOA Editions, 2013), won the James Laughlin Award from the Academy of American Poets. She teaches at Clemson University.*